JUMBLE®

Jambalaya

Stir Up Some Jumble Fun!

Henri Arnold, Bob Lee, and Mike Argirion

TRIUMPH
BOOKS

This book is available in quantity at special discounts
for your group or organization.

For further information, contact:

Triumph Books
814 North Franklin Street
Chicago, Illinois 60610
(312) 337-0747
www.triumphbooks.com

Printed in U.S.A.

ISBN: 978-1-60078-294-7

Design by Sue Knopf

CONTENTS

JUMBLE®

Jambalaya

Classic Puzzles

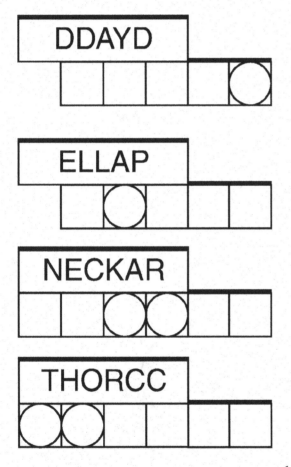

JUMBLE®

Unscramble these four Jumbles, one letter to each square, to form four ordinary words.

DDAYD

ELLAP

NECKAR

THORCC

BACK THEN, WHEN THE AUTO WOULDN'T START, THE DRIVER BECAME----

Now arrange the circled letters to form the surprise answer, as suggested by the above cartoon.

Print answer here   "◯◯◯◯◯◯"

JUMBLE®

Unscramble these four Jumbles, one letter to each square, to form four ordinary words.

TUFOL

CONIT

TRAPIE

MURTES

He's always perfectly groomed

He's very mysterious

NOBODY KNEW THE SPY WORE A TOUPEE BECAUSE IT WAS---

Now arrange the circled letters to form the surprise answer, as suggested by the above cartoon.

Print answer here " ◯◯◯ " ◯◯◯◯◯◯◯

JUMBLE®

Unscramble these four Jumbles, one letter to each square, to form four ordinary words.

UCLID

LYPHS

LADUFE

TWERPE

...and I'll also cut taxes to the bone

He's got my vote

WHEN HE PROMISED THIS, THE TAILOR RUNNING FOR OFFICE---

Now arrange the circled letters to form the surprise answer, as suggested by the above cartoon.

Print answer here " ⬡⬡⬡⬡⬡ " IT ⬡⬡

JUMBLE®

Unscramble these four Jumbles, one letter to each square, to form four ordinary words.

DYRYL

OAKEW

DARAMA

INMOOT

...and at 8 o'clock traffic is...

WHAT HE HAD ON WHEN HE WAS AWAKENED.

Now arrange the circled letters to form the surprise answer, as suggested by the above cartoon.

Print answer here **A**

5

JUMBLE®

Unscramble these four Jumbles, one letter to each square, to form four ordinary words.

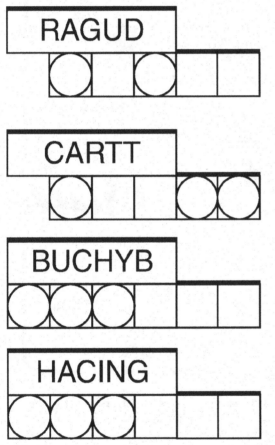

RAGUD

CARTT

BUCHYB

HACING

Attaboy, Stevie

You're late. Almost missed it

WHEN DAD ARRIVED IN TIME TO SEE HIS SON'S SPEC-TACULAR PLAY, HE———

Now arrange the circled letters to form the surprise answer, as suggested by the above cartoon.

Print answer here "⬡⬡⬡⬡⬡⬡⬡" THE ⬡⬡⬡⬡⬡

JUMBLE®

Unscramble these four Jumbles, one letter to each square, to form four ordinary words.

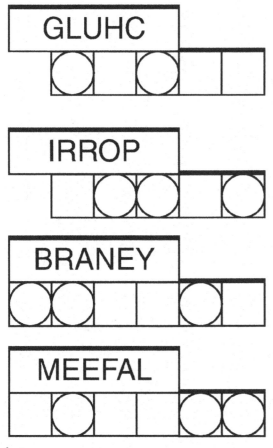

GLUHC

IRROP

BRANEY

MEEFAL

Tomorrow we'll start looking for dishes, and then...

WHEN HE GOT ENGAGED, HE BECAME ----

Now arrange the circled letters to form the surprise answer, as suggested by the above cartoon.

Print answer here **A**

JUMBLE®

Unscramble these four Jumbles, one letter to each square, to form four ordinary words.

IMNEC

ADEHA

GETURT

PHANEP

Struck him out

We win

He's number one in my book

8

MGR

THE MANAGER SAID THE WINNING SOUTH-PAW WAS HIS----

Now arrange the circled letters to form the surprise answer, as suggested by the above cartoon.

Print answer here

JUMBLE®

Unscramble these four Jumbles, one letter to
each square, to form four ordinary words.

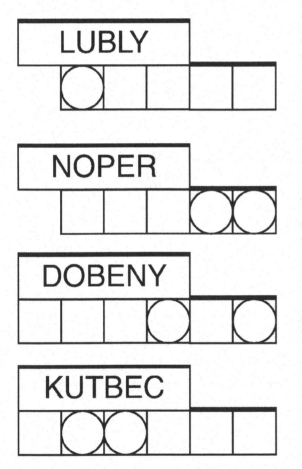

LUBLY

NOPER

DOBENY

KUTBEC

That's it.
You're through

WHEN THE JUGGLER
KEPT DROPPING THE
BALL, HE WAS——

Now arrange the circled letters to form the
surprise answer, as suggested by the above
cartoon.

Print answer here " ◯◯◯◯◯◯◯ "

JUMBLE®

Unscramble these four Jumbles, one letter to each square, to form four ordinary words.

SHEWO

ALVAN

ANNAAB

MOPSIE

These are for you, Mrs. Smith

Oh, how thoughtful

WHAT SHE HOPED HER MOTHER WOULD GET WHEN HER NEW BEAU CAME CALLING.

Now arrange the circled letters to form the surprise answer, as suggested by the above cartoon.

Print answer here A

JUMBLE

Unscramble these four Jumbles, one letter to each square, to form four ordinary words.

NOKTE

RODUG

REBISC

HOYBIS

I'll take these, and I also need new soles and heels

HOW THE REPAIR SHOP MADE MONEY SELLING LACES.

Now arrange the circled letters to form the surprise answer, as suggested by the above cartoon.

Print answer here ON A ⬜⬜⬜⬜⬜⬜⬜⬜⬜⬜⬜

JUMBLE®

Unscramble these four Jumbles, one letter to each square, to form four ordinary words.

MILIT

PUDMY

HUCNAH

GENJAL

That
one
is cute

What about
the hunk
over there?

WHAT THE FEMALE DETECTIVES CON- DUCTED AT THE SINGLES BAR.

Now arrange the circled letters to form the surprise answer, as suggested by the above cartoon.

Print answer here A

JUMBLE®

Unscramble these four Jumbles, one letter to each square, to form four ordinary words.

WARLC

ADDEJ

BALTOC

MYCALL

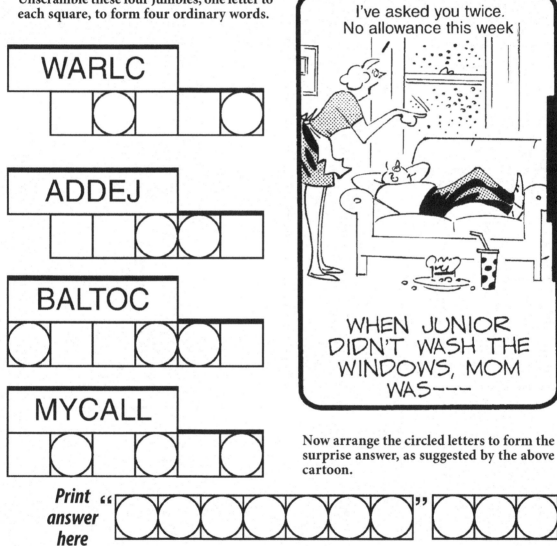

I've asked you twice.
No allowance this week

WHEN JUNIOR
DIDN'T WASH THE
WINDOWS, MOM
WAS---

Now arrange the circled letters to form the surprise answer, as suggested by the above cartoon.

Print answer here "◯◯◯◯◯◯◯" ◯◯◯

JUMBLE®

Unscramble these four Jumbles, one letter to each square, to form four ordinary words.

DUFIL

PREKO

DUPLED

YALDDE

Hey! What's going on?

I guess he was thirsty

WHAT THE GREY-HOUND DID DURING THE RACE.

Now arrange the circled letters to form the surprise answer, as suggested by the above cartoon.

Print answer here " ⬭⬭⬭⬭⬭ " **THE** ⬭⬭⬭⬭⬭

JUMBLE®

Unscramble these four Jumbles, one letter to each square, to form four ordinary words.

LASIA

NEKEL

LAURIB

LAPPOR

These will yield a lot of roasts

EASY FOR PIG FARMERS TO GROW.

Now arrange the circled letters to form the surprise answer, as suggested by the above cartoon.

Print answer here

15

JUMBLE®

Unscramble these four Jumbles, one letter to each square, to form four ordinary words.

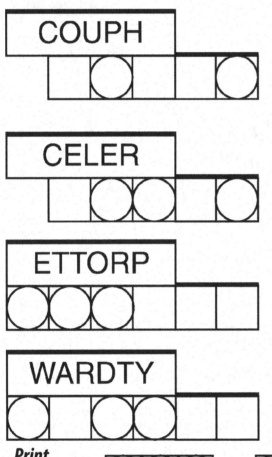

COUPH

CELER

ETTORP

WARDTY

The people are so friendly

I haven't felt so relaxed in years

HOW THEY FELT WHEN THEY TOOK A TRIP DOWN UNDER.

Now arrange the circled letters to form the surprise answer, as suggested by the above cartoon.

Print answer here ON ☐◯◯◯ OF ☐◯◯◯ ◯◯◯◯◯

JUMBLE®

Unscramble these four Jumbles, one letter to each square, to form four ordinary words.

IDDEC

PYPIN

HARTOX

PERRIM

The abdomen really fascinates me

THE MEDICAL STUDENT'S FAVOR- ITE SECTION IN THE TEXTBOOK.

Now arrange the circled letters to form the surprise answer, as suggested by the above cartoon.

Print answer here THE

JUMBLE®

Unscramble these four Jumbles, one letter to
each square, to form four ordinary words.

HORTT

GEFUD

GOLLAB

ERTOPY

I find
these
fascinating

Uggh!

WHY HE STARTED
STUDYING INSECTS.

Now arrange the circled letters to form the
surprise answer, as suggested by the above
cartoon.

*Print
answer
here* HE

JUMBLE®

Unscramble these four Jumbles, one letter to
each square, to form four ordinary words.

MYLOD

HEANN

ONDUBA

BLAURT

Helps keep
me warm

Better let me
hold the gun

AFTER A FEW
DRINKS, THE
HUNTER AND HIS
RIFLE WERE----

Now arrange the circled letters to form the
surprise answer, as suggested by the above
cartoon.

*Print
answer
here*

19

JUMBLE®

Unscramble these four Jumbles, one letter to each square, to form four ordinary words.

NORCO

YOPPP

PEKUPE

BREMME

Are they made of gold?

I think they're becoming

WHEN HE GOT THE BILL FOR HER NEW GLASSES, IT WAS----

Now arrange the circled letters to form the surprise answer, as suggested by the above cartoon.

Print answer here **AN** ☐☐☐-☐☐☐☐☐☐☐

JUMBLE®

Unscramble these four Jumbles, one letter to each square, to form four ordinary words.

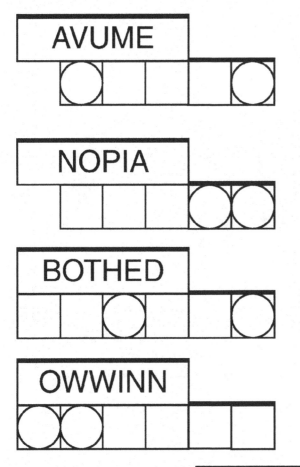

AVUME

NOPIA

BOTHED

OWWINN

I can hardly see straight. I need a nap

Let's play

WHAT DAD NEEDED AFTER SITTING AT THE COMPUTER FOR HOURS.

Now arrange the circled letters to form the surprise answer, as suggested by the above cartoon.

Print answer here " ◯◯◯◯ " ◯◯◯◯

JUMBLE®

Unscramble these four Jumbles, one letter to each square, to form four ordinary words.

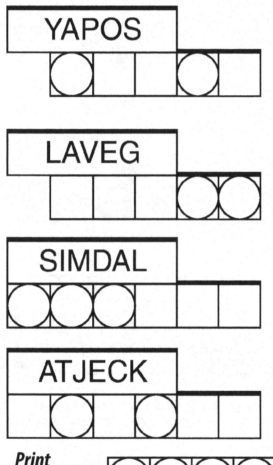

YAPOS

LAVEG

SIMDAL

ATJECK

Three spades

Four hearts

Umm...I'm not sure

WHY THE QUARTER-BACK WAS A LOUSY BRIDGE PLAYER.

Now arrange the circled letters to form the surprise answer, as suggested by the above cartoon.

Print answer here HE ◯◯◯◯◯ TO "◯◯◯◯"

JUMBLE®

Unscramble these four Jumbles, one letter to each square, to form four ordinary words.

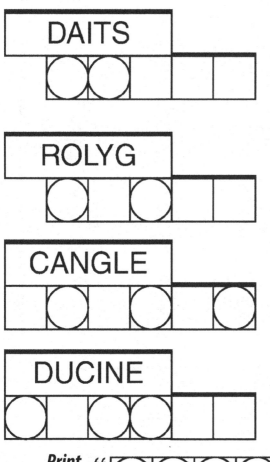

DAITS

ROLYG

CANGLE

DUCINE

I'm more nervous than the groom

He's not married, you know

WHEN THE BEST MAN MADE A TOAST, HE WAS----

Now arrange the circled letters to form the surprise answer, as suggested by the above cartoon.

Print answer here " _____ " ___

JUMBLE®

Unscramble these four Jumbles, one letter to each square, to form four ordinary words.

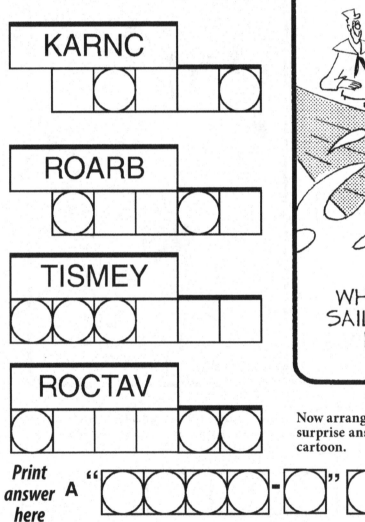

KARNC

ROARB

TISMEY

ROCTAV

He needs his sea legs

WHAT THE NEW SAILOR HAD ON HIS FIRST VOYAGE.

Now arrange the circled letters to form the surprise answer, as suggested by the above cartoon.

Print answer here **A** " ⬭⬭⬭⬭-⬭ " ⬭⬭⬭⬭⬭

JUMBLE®

Unscramble these four Jumbles, one letter to each square, to form four ordinary words.

WICTE

YONIR

NAITED

CULIES

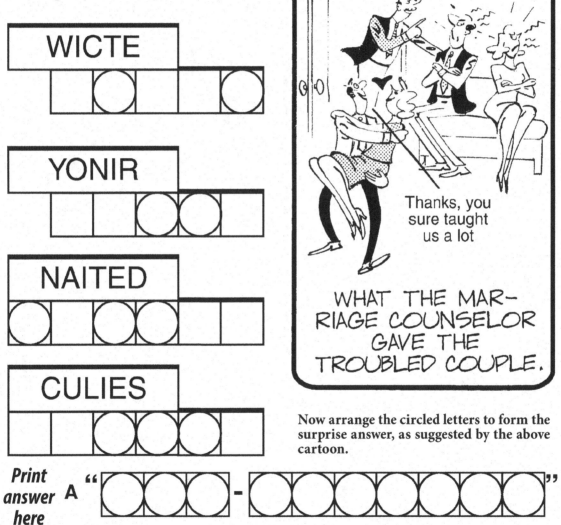

Next

Thanks, you sure taught us a lot

WHAT THE MAR-RIAGE COUNSELOR GAVE THE TROUBLED COUPLE.

Now arrange the circled letters to form the surprise answer, as suggested by the above cartoon.

Print answer here

A "⬡⬡⬡-⬡⬡⬡⬡⬡⬡⬡"

JUMBLE®

Unscramble these four Jumbles, one letter to
each square, to form four ordinary words.

CHOPE

KILSY

UNJELG

YONTUB

If it gives me any
problems, Mac,
I'll be back

SOLD

WHEN THE BRAWLER
BOUGHT A PRE-
OWNED CAR, THE
SALESMAN SAID
HE WAS----

Now arrange the circled letters to form the
surprise answer, as suggested by the above
cartoon.

Print answer
here **A** " ⬡⬡⬡⬡⬡ " ⬡⬡⬡⬡

JUMBLE®

Jambalaya

Daily
Puzzles

JUMBLE®

Unscramble these four Jumbles, one letter to each square, to form four ordinary words.

WARLD

LEELB

TOWPUN

KLINTE

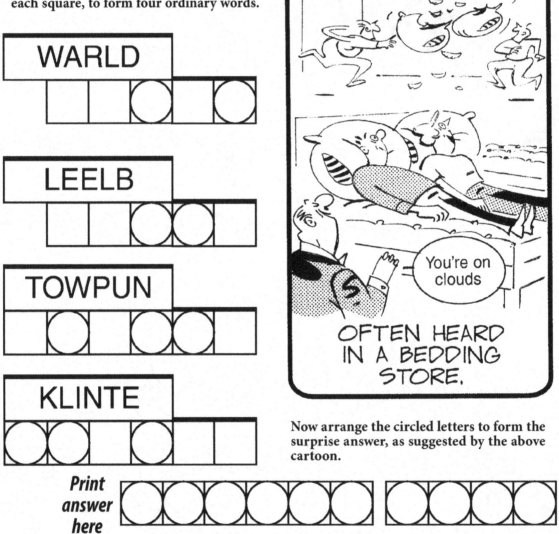

You're on clouds

OFTEN HEARD IN A BEDDING STORE.

Now arrange the circled letters to form the surprise answer, as suggested by the above cartoon.

Print answer here

JUMBLE®

Unscramble these four Jumbles, one letter to
each square, to form four ordinary words.

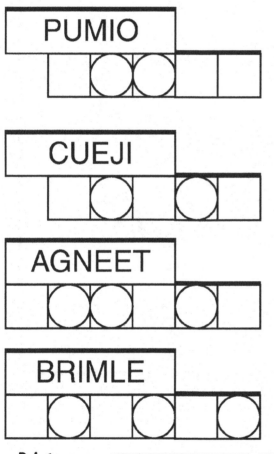

PUMIO

CUEJI

AGNEET

BRIMLE

Hmmm...could
use a dab
of red in
that corner

WHAT THE MURAL-
IST FOCUSED ON
WHEN HE COM-
PLETED HIS WORK.

Now arrange the circled letters to form the
surprise answer, as suggested by the above
cartoon.

*Print
answer
here* THE

29

JUMBLE®

Unscramble these four Jumbles, one letter to each square, to form four ordinary words.

TINGY

DANGL

HARTTO

GNININ

A perfect end to our vacation

How romantic

A BEAUTIFUL SUN-SET MAKES A DIF-FERENCE IN THIS.

Now arrange the circled letters to form the surprise answer, as suggested by the above cartoon.

Print answer here ◯◯◯ **AND** ◯◯◯◯◯

JUMBLE®

Unscramble these four Jumbles, one letter to each square, to form four ordinary words.

NEKIF

TOAQU

KAJLAC

YARDOP

HAPPY BIRTHDAY!

WHAT THE DOG CATCHER GOT ON HIS BIRTHDAY.

Now arrange the circled letters to form the surprise answer, as suggested by the above cartoon.

Print answer here " ⬯⬯⬯⬯⬯ " ⬯⬯⬯⬯

JUMBLE®

Unscramble these four Jumbles, one letter to each square, to form four ordinary words.

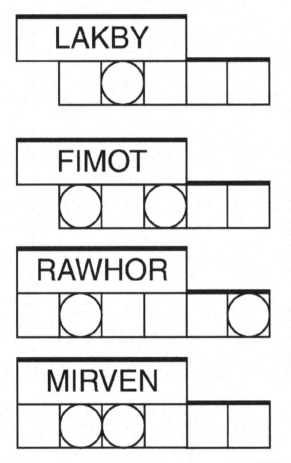

LAKBY

FIMOT

RAWHOR

MIRVEN

May I recommend the buffalo steak?

SOLD IN BUTCHER SHOPS BUT SEL-DOM SERVED IN RESTAURANTS.

Now arrange the circled letters to form the surprise answer, as suggested by the above cartoon.

 *Print answer here*

JUMBLE®

Unscramble these four Jumbles, one letter to each square, to form four ordinary words.

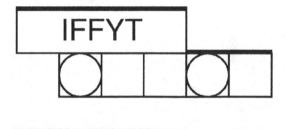
IFFYT

CIENE

LAUTRI

RUVESS

BAR

Only three hours left

So many bars, so little time

TWENTY-FOUR HOURS ON SHORE GAVE THE SAILORS THIS.

Now arrange the circled letters to form the surprise answer, as suggested by the above cartoon.

Print answer A here

 " ◯◯◯◯◯ " ◯◯◯◯◯

JUMBLE®

Unscramble these four Jumbles, one letter to each square, to form four ordinary words.

EFNOL

GANET

GUMPSY

NOMOIK

It wasn't me. It was that infamous feather gang

WHAT HE TURNED INTO WHEN THE EXOTIC BIRDS WERE STOLEN.

Now arrange the circled letters to form the surprise answer, as suggested by the above cartoon.

Print answer here A

JUMBLE®

Unscramble these four Jumbles, one letter to each square, to form four ordinary words.

GEITH

OUDES

PACTER

GURDED

Congratulations

Hmph! Not bad for a mongrel

WHEN ROVER FINISHED OBEDI-ENCE SCHOOL, HE HAD A ---

Now arrange the circled letters to form the surprise answer, as suggested by the above cartoon.

Print answer here " ◯◯◯ - ◯◯◯◯◯◯◯ "

JUMBLE®

Unscramble these four Jumbles, one letter to each square, to form four ordinary words.

DENIK

ROGOF

KOHOED

PICTES

Outta my way!

After you, sir

IT OFTEN TAKES THIS TO PUT UP WITH BAD MANNERS.

Now arrange the circled letters to form the surprise answer, as suggested by the above cartoon.

Print answer here

JUMBLE®

Unscramble these four Jumbles, one letter to
each square, to form four ordinary words.

TULIQ

HYSOW

NAITAT

CALPEA

You guys are
the worst

WHEN THE QUICK
TIRE CHANGE WAS
BOTCHED, THE
RACER SAID HIS
LOSS WAS---

Now arrange the circled letters to form the
surprise answer, as suggested by the above
cartoon.

Print answer here ◯◯◯ " ◯◯◯◯ "

37

JUMBLE®

Unscramble these four Jumbles, one letter to
each square, to form four ordinary words.

LICCO

BEATA

ENKASH

PATTOE

WHAT DAD DID
WHILE WATCHING
THE PET SHOW.

Now arrange the circled letters to form the
surprise answer, as suggested by the above
cartoon.

**Print
answer
here**

A

JUMBLE®

Unscramble these four Jumbles, one letter to each square, to form four ordinary words.

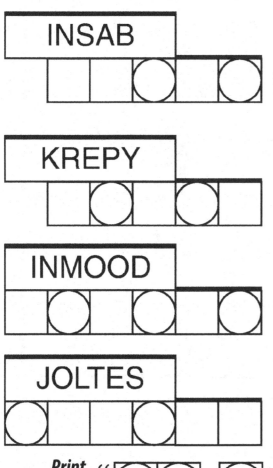

INSAB

KREPY

INMOOD

JOLTES

Sorry, folks, no show tonight

I'm suing

I want my money back

WHEN THE COMEDIAN FAILED TO APPEAR, THE NIGHTCLUB OWNER SAID—––

Now arrange the circled letters to form the surprise answer, as suggested by the above cartoon.

Print answer here

" ⬡⬡ ' ⬡ ⬡⬡ ⬡⬡⬡⬡ "

JUMBLE®

Unscramble these four Jumbles, one letter to each square, to form four ordinary words.

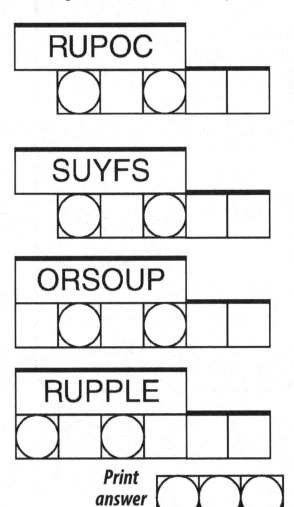

RUPOC

SUYFS

ORSOUP

RUPPLE

I want an exclusive... how has the economy affected sales?

65 FLAVORS

WHY THE REPORTER VISITED THE ICE-CREAM PARLOR.

Now arrange the circled letters to form the surprise answer, as suggested by the above cartoon.

Print answer here

A " "

JUMBLE®

Unscramble these four Jumbles, one letter to each square, to form four ordinary words.

NAWTY

NOVEM

AEDING

YESWIL

It's not moving

Everybody stay calm

WHEN THE ELEVATOR GOT STUCK ON THE WAY UP, THE RIDERS SAID---

Now arrange the circled letters to form the surprise answer, as suggested by the above cartoon.

Print answer here IT ◯◯◯ "◯◯◯◯"

JUMBLE®

Unscramble these four Jumbles, one letter to each square, to form four ordinary words.

SHACO

SCERS

DECORF

INGUMP

You've gained ten pounds

My clothes will fit, but I'll miss my candy

WHAT SHE "WEIGHED" BEFORE STARTING HER DIET.

Now arrange the circled letters to form the surprise answer, as suggested by the above cartoon.

Print answer here THE ⭕⭕⭕⭕⭕ AND ⭕⭕⭕⭕⭕

JUMBLE®

Unscramble these four Jumbles, one letter to
each square, to form four ordinary words.

HAKSY

BYASS

GINMOH

WHEPEN

He's terrific at this

Whatcha
doin'
tonight,
honey?

THE QUARTERBACK
PURSUING THE
CHEERLEADER WAS
NOTED FOR---

Now arrange the circled letters to form the
surprise answer, as suggested by the above
cartoon.

*Print
answer
here*   " "

JUMBLE®

Unscramble these four Jumbles, one letter to each square, to form four ordinary words.

TAFAL

BOAVE

GROOFT

REKALT

I think I'll skip it

C'mon you'll be fine

WHAT THE NERVOUS FLYER WANTED TO DO AS DEPARTURE TIME NEARED.

Now arrange the circled letters to form the surprise answer, as suggested by the above cartoon.

Print answer here

JUMBLE®

Unscramble these four Jumbles, one letter to each square, to form four ordinary words.

GIMED

TANCH

LAUTAC

DEGELP

I can't... too many calories

Relax, a bite won't hurt

GOOD ADVICE FOR AN OBSESSIVE DIETER.

Now arrange the circled letters to form the surprise answer, as suggested by the above cartoon.

Print answer here " ◯◯◯◯◯◯◯ " ◯◯

JUMBLE®

Unscramble these four Jumbles, one letter to each square, to form four ordinary words.

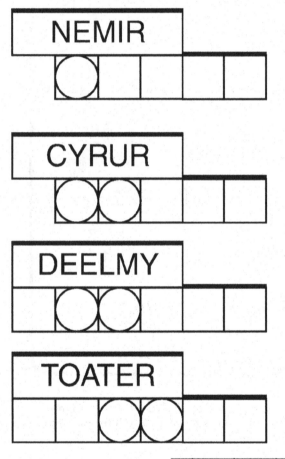

NEMIR

CYRUR

DEELMY

TOATER

I'll take Sam. He did the best job

WHAT THE TOUR GOLFER-TURNED-BUTCHER DID.

Now arrange the circled letters to form the surprise answer, as suggested by the above cartoon.

Print answer here ⬡⬡⬡⬡ THE " ⬡⬡⬡ "

JUMBLE®

Unscramble these four Jumbles, one letter to each square, to form four ordinary words.

USVEA

ZIPER

COZADI

HETOLC

I'm so tired I can't see straight

I'm going to sleep for a week

SILENCE

WHAT THEY FACED WHEN THEY STUDIED FOR FINAL EXAMS.

Now arrange the circled letters to form the surprise answer, as suggested by the above cartoon.

Print answer here

" "

JUMBLE®

Unscramble these four Jumbles, one letter to
each square, to form four ordinary words.

ENCAP

RAMEF

YEEHRB

TUITOW

Therefore, the answer is...

Brilliant

$$2\pi R = C$$
$$2\pi (R+1-D$$
$$2\pi R \cdot 2\pi H$$
$$= 2 \times 3.14 =$$
$$h = 3.$$

WHAT THE PRO-
FESSOR CONSIDERED
THE STUDENT'S
SOLUTION TO
THE EQUATION.

Now arrange the circled letters to form the
surprise answer, as suggested by the above
cartoon.

*Print
answer
here* A " ⬡⬡⬡⬡⬡ - ⬡⬡⬡⬡⬡⬡⬡⬡ "

48

JUMBLE®

Unscramble these four Jumbles, one letter to
each square, to form four ordinary words.

RASEE

DURIL

ZULZEG

TREVIN

I can't bear to look

WHEN HE TRIED
TO HANG WALL-
PAPER, SHE
BECAME---

Now arrange the circled letters to form the
surprise answer, as suggested by the above
cartoon.

Print answer here

JUMBLE®

Unscramble these four Jumbles, one letter to each square, to form four ordinary words.

KLUSK

ESHOU

WENITH

DYLOOB

WHEN THE FIGHT WAS OVER, THE BOXER ENDED UP LICKING——

Now arrange the circled letters to form the surprise answer, as suggested by the above cartoon.

Print answer here

JUMBLE®

Unscramble these four Jumbles, one letter to
each square, to form four ordinary words.

CINIG

TESCA

WILDEM

RYNWIT

ACME
PRETZEL
CO.

Any
bright
ideas?

NEEDED BY THE
PRETZEL MAKERS
TO INCREASE
SALES.

Now arrange the circled letters to form the
surprise answer, as suggested by the above
cartoon.

Print answer here **A** ◯◯◯ " ◯◯◯◯◯ "

JUMBLE®

Unscramble these four Jumbles, one letter to each square, to form four ordinary words.

REEMY

WODDY

INTIEF

POWNEA

Feel free to come in at any time

THE BOSS NEVER CLOSED HIS OFFICE DOOR BECAUSE HE WAS---

Now arrange the circled letters to form the surprise answer, as suggested by the above cartoon.

Print answer here " _ _ _ _ "   _ _ _ _ _ _

JUMBLE®

Unscramble these four Jumbles, one letter to each square, to form four ordinary words.

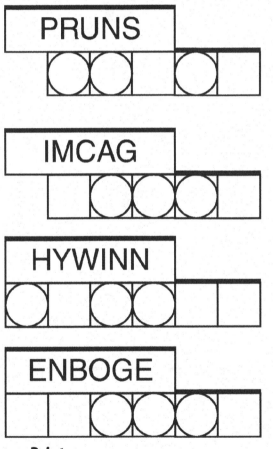

PRUNS

IMCAG

HYWINN

ENBOGE

Whew, I'm sore all over

We'll be picking corn soon

WHAT THE TEEN-AGER EXPERIENCED ON THE FARM.

Now arrange the circled letters to form the surprise answer, as suggested by the above cartoon.

Print answer here "⬡⬡⬡⬡⬡⬡⬡" ⬡⬡⬡⬡⬡

JUMBLE

Unscramble these four Jumbles, one letter to each square, to form four ordinary words.

WEJEL

BITHA

UNLACH

LOMBIE

It's not straight

WHERE THE ASSIS-
TANT ENDED UP
WHEN THE DOOR
WOULDN'T FIT.

Now arrange the circled letters to form the surprise answer, as suggested by the above cartoon.

Print answer here ⬡⬡ A " ⬡⬡⬡⬡ "

JUMBLE®

Unscramble these four Jumbles, one letter to each square, to form four ordinary words.

SIVOR

SURVI

RUIPFY

TELTAC

"#$%!! It's driving me nuts

WHAT CITIZENS TURN INTO AT TAX TIME.

Now arrange the circled letters to form the surprise answer, as suggested by the above cartoon.

Print answer here " ☐☐☐ - ☐☐☐☐☐☐ "

JUMBLE®

Unscramble these four Jumbles, one letter to
each square, to form four ordinary words.

ZUZYF

BOREP

INLARM

EXTUDO

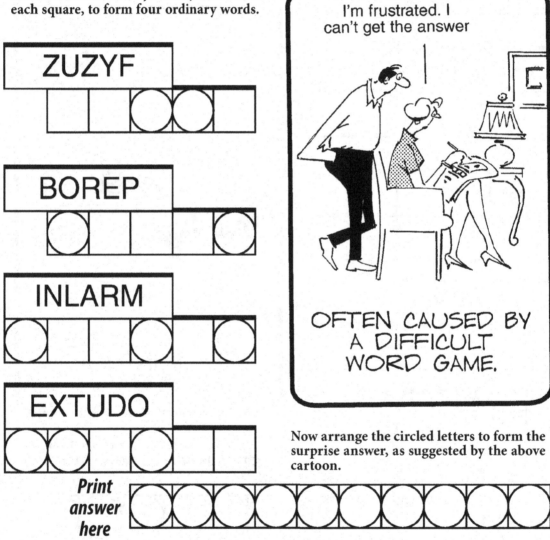

I'm frustrated. I
can't get the answer

OFTEN CAUSED BY
A DIFFICULT
WORD GAME.

Now arrange the circled letters to form the
surprise answer, as suggested by the above
cartoon.

*Print
answer
here*

JUMBLE®

Unscramble these four Jumbles, one letter to
each square, to form four ordinary words.

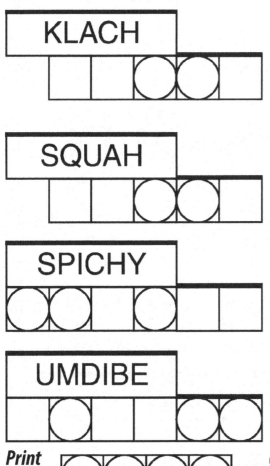

KLACH

SQUAH

SPICHY

UMDIBE

Omigosh, isn't that...?

It'll be
all over
the papers
and TV

WHAT THE MOVIE
STAR DID WHEN
SHE DIVED
INTO THE POOL.

Now arrange the circled letters to form the
surprise answer, as suggested by the above
cartoon.

*Print
answer
here*

A "   "

JUMBLE®

Unscramble these four Jumbles, one letter to each square, to form four ordinary words.

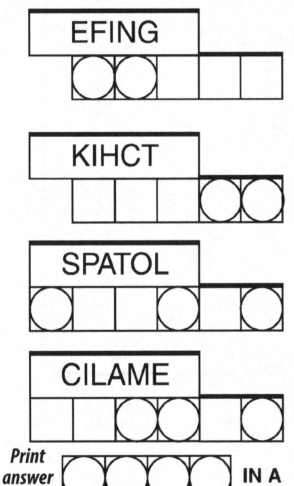

EFING

KIHCT

SPATOL

CILAME

How am I going to put up all these cucumbers?

WHEN GRANDMA RAN OUT OF JARS, SHE WAS----

Now arrange the circled letters to form the surprise answer, as suggested by the above cartoon.

Print answer here

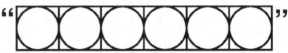

IN A " "

JUMBLE®

Unscramble these four Jumbles, one letter to each square, to form four ordinary words.

LIQUA

PEELO

TORICE

LARFOL

I've got to send out invitations, buy the food, set the table, do the cleaning...

WHAT THE HOSTESS FACED BEFORE THE DINNER PARTY.

Now arrange the circled letters to form the surprise answer, as suggested by the above cartoon.

Print answer here **A**

JUMBLE

Unscramble these four Jumbles, one letter to each square, to form four ordinary words.

YONEH

ROVLE

RUTSLY

ROVEXT

He is honest and his work is perfect

Hmm--just a little off

THE CARPENTER WAS HIGHLY RECOMMENDED BECAUSE HE WAS STRICTLY---

Now arrange the circled letters to form the surprise answer, as suggested by the above cartoon.

Print answer here **ON** ☐☐☐ " ☐☐☐☐☐ "

JUMBLE®

Unscramble these four Jumbles, one letter to
each square, to form four ordinary words.

RIPEV

SELOU

HERLAW

TEICED

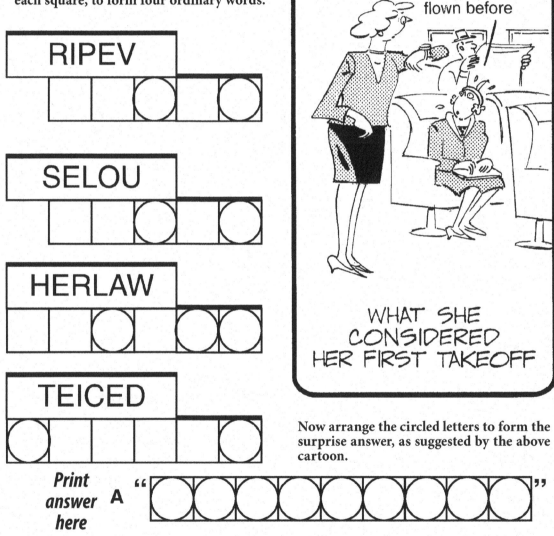

I've never
flown before

WHAT SHE
CONSIDERED
HER FIRST TAKEOFF

Now arrange the circled letters to form the
surprise answer, as suggested by the above
cartoon.

*Print
answer
here* A "⬭⬭⬭⬭⬭⬭⬭⬭⬭⬭"

JUMBLE®

Unscramble these four Jumbles, one letter to
each square, to form four ordinary words.

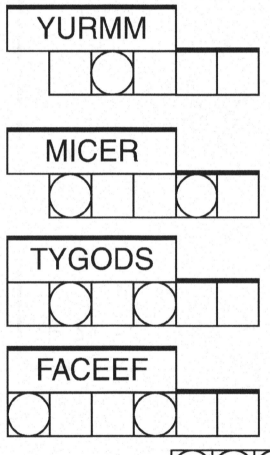

YURMM

MICER

TYGODS

FACEEF

We only offer a position to
one of twenty candidates

WHY THE YOUNG
SURGEON WAS
HIRED.

Now arrange the circled letters to form the
surprise answer, as suggested by the above
cartoon.

Print answer here   HE ⬡⬡⬡⬡⬡ THE "⬡⬡⬡"

JUMBLE®

Unscramble these four Jumbles, one letter to each square, to form four ordinary words.

WETET

STEAE

TRAINO

CALBEM

Yuch! I'm not buying here anymore

$4 POUND
$8 POUND

WHAT THE PAT-RONS WERE LEFT WITH WHEN THE SWEETSHOP RAISED PRICES.

Now arrange the circled letters to form the surprise answer, as suggested by the above cartoon.

Print answer here **A** " ◯◯◯◯◯◯ " ◯◯◯◯◯

JUMBLE®

Unscramble these four Jumbles, one letter to each square, to form four ordinary words.

SMACH

LAVIA

ELYSEP

RATHEG

Take a seat. You're out of the game

WHAT THE COACH DID TO THE END WHO MISSED THE CATCH.

Now arrange the circled letters to form the surprise answer, as suggested by the above cartoon.

Print answer here

A " "

JUMBLE®

Unscramble these four Jumbles, one letter to each square, to form four ordinary words.

ANIFT

FEZOR

DIMRAY

GURMOE

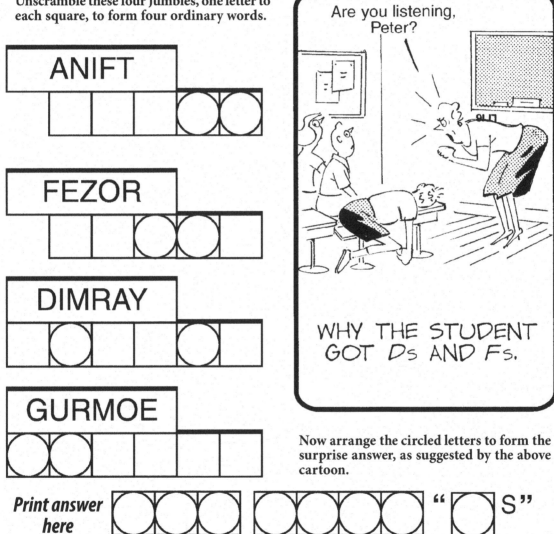

Are you listening, Peter?

WHY THE STUDENT GOT Ds AND Fs.

Now arrange the circled letters to form the surprise answer, as suggested by the above cartoon.

Print answer here ⬡⬡⬡ ⬡⬡⬡⬡ " ⬡ S "

JUMBLE®

Unscramble these four Jumbles, one letter to each square, to form four ordinary words.

CHOVA

ORFID

MASHAT

CROSCH

These pine branches will keep out the cold

WHAT THE STRANDED CAMPERS USED TO STAY WARM.

Now arrange the circled letters to form the surprise answer, as suggested by the above cartoon.

Print answer here A " ◯◯◯ " ◯◯◯◯

JUMBLE®

Unscramble these four Jumbles, one letter to
each square, to form four ordinary words.

BILLE

CENOU

NEDDAW

HUBERC

My next project is
Asian cooking

STUDYING CULINARY
ARTS MADE HIM
THIS.

Now arrange the circled letters to form the
surprise answer, as suggested by the above
cartoon.

**Print
answer
here** ◯◯◯◯◯ " ◯◯◯◯◯◯◯◯ "

JUMBLE®

Unscramble these four Jumbles, one letter to
each square, to form four ordinary words.

VUCER

ZYZID

CARAFS

DENGER

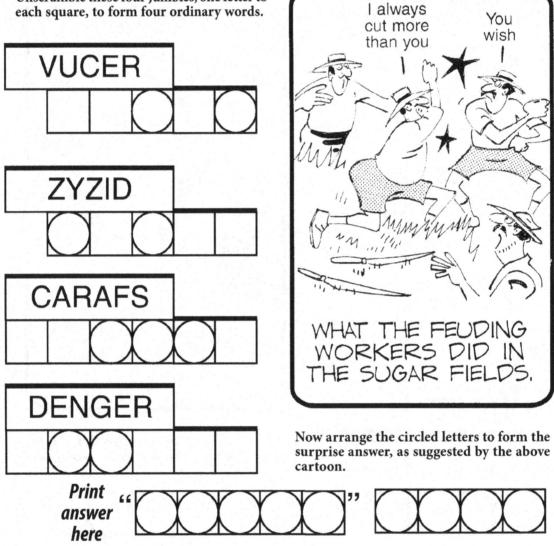

I always
cut more
than you

You
wish

WHAT THE FEUDING
WORKERS DID IN
THE SUGAR FIELDS.

Now arrange the circled letters to form the
surprise answer, as suggested by the above
cartoon.

*Print
answer
here* " ☐☐☐☐☐ " ☐☐☐☐

JUMBLE®

Unscramble these four Jumbles, one letter to
each square, to form four ordinary words.

GUPER

ATAGE

YIPLOC

FRODIL

You cut it
too short

That'll be
40 bucks

WHY HE DECIDED
TO CHANGE
BARBERS.

Now arrange the circled letters to form the
surprise answer, as suggested by the above
cartoon.

**Print
answer
here** HE ⟨ ⟩⟨ ⟩⟨ ⟩ " ⟨ ⟩⟨ ⟩⟨ ⟩⟨ ⟩⟨ ⟩⟨ ⟩⟨ ⟩⟨ ⟩ "

JUMBLE®

Unscramble these four Jumbles, one letter to
each square, to form four ordinary words.

BEREL

ROFUL

GUYSAR

WORMAR

Use plenty
of disinfectant

WHAT THE TROOPS
CONDUCTED DURING
BARRACKS CLEANUP.

Now arrange the circled letters to form the
surprise answer, as suggested by the above
cartoon.

*Print
answer
here*   " ⬡⬡⬡⬡ "   ⬡⬡⬡⬡⬡⬡⬡

JUMBLE®

Unscramble these four Jumbles, one letter to each square, to form four ordinary words.

CHEFT

BRIHC

REDUNE

TUGELL

I'm happy but hoarse

My throat is raw

AFTER THE VICTORY, THE POM-POM GIRLS WERE---

Now arrange the circled letters to form the surprise answer, as suggested by the above cartoon.

Print answer here " ☐☐☐☐☐ " ☐☐☐☐

JUMBLE®

Unscramble these four Jumbles, one letter to each square, to form four ordinary words.

WARBL

PODOR

BINBBO

LEUXED

I'll never get out of here on time

HOW THE SHIPPING CLERK FELT ON AN ESPECIALLY BUSY DAY.

Now arrange the circled letters to form the surprise answer, as suggested by the above cartoon.

Print answer here " ◯◯◯◯◯ " ◯◯

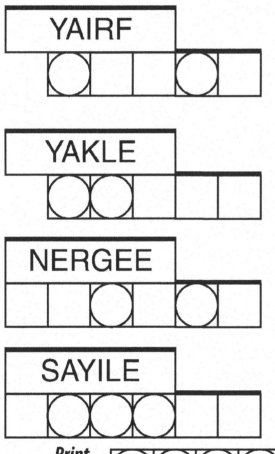

JUMBLE®

Unscramble these four Jumbles, one letter to
each square, to form four ordinary words.

YAIRF

YAKLE

NERGEE

SAYILE

Congratulations! You've
won a 10-day vacation if...

CLICK

HE HUNG UP ON
THE TELEMARKETER
BECAUSE HIS
SALES PITCH
HAD A---

Now arrange the circled letters to form the
surprise answer, as suggested by the above
cartoon.

*Print
answer
here*

" "

JUMBLE®

Unscramble these four Jumbles, one letter to each square, to form four ordinary words.

ESSOU

PRUPE

TAPHAY

TIPECK

This ride saves me hours

How's the mileage?

WHAT THE TIMBER BOSS TOOK TO WORK.

Now arrange the circled letters to form the surprise answer, as suggested by the above cartoon.

Print answer here   HIS "⬡⬡⬡⬡⬡⬡⬡⬡"

JUMBLE

Unscramble these four Jumbles, one letter to each square, to form four ordinary words.

LECEX

TULOC

VARSOY

TOPECK

And I just had it checked

Of all the times..!

HARD TO DO WHEN THE AIR CONDITIONER GOES OUT ON A HOT DAY.

Now arrange the circled letters to form the surprise answer, as suggested by the above cartoon.

Print answer here

[   ] [   ] [   ] [   ] [   ] "[   ] [   ] [   ] [   ]"

JUMBLE®

Unscramble these four Jumbles, one letter to
each square, to form four ordinary words.

GIRRO

WONIG

TOBUNT

LANTUF

Ouch! You did it again

HOW CLOSE DID
THE COUPLE COME
TO WINNING THE
DANCE CONTEST?

Now arrange the circled letters to form the
surprise answer, as suggested by the above
cartoon.

Print answer here **A** " ⬭⬭⬭⬭ " **OR** ⬭⬭⬭

JUMBLE®

Unscramble these four Jumbles, one letter to each square, to form four ordinary words.

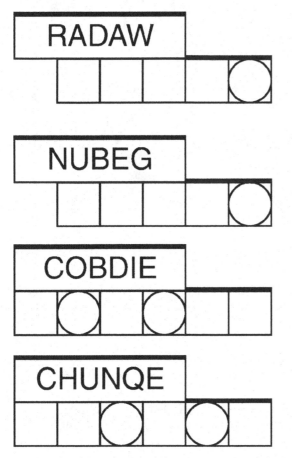

RADAW

NUBEG

COBDIE

CHUNQE

C'mon, seven

Gambling isn't allowed, gentlemen

WHAT THE MANA-
GER SAID WHEN
THE CLUB MEMBERS
PLAYED CRAPS.

Now arrange the circled letters to form the surprise answer, as suggested by the above cartoon.

Print answer here " ⬜⬜ ⬜⬜⬜⬜ "

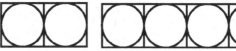

JUMBLE®

Unscramble these four Jumbles, one letter to each square, to form four ordinary words.

YAMOF

KYSHU

COTESK

CUTOLC

Buy it right now, and I'll save you $2000

SALE

THE SALESMAN GAVE THE CUSTOMER A HARD SELL BECAUSE HE WAS----

Now arrange the circled letters to form the surprise answer, as suggested by the above cartoon.

Print answer here A

JUMBLE®

Unscramble these four Jumbles, one letter to each square, to form four ordinary words.

VALEE

AUPSE

NADDIC

YEMMAH

Buy the powder, and I'll give you the brush and eye shadow

WHAT THE COSMETICS SALESWOMAN GAVE THE MOBSTER'S WIFE.

Now arrange the circled letters to form the surprise answer, as suggested by the above cartoon.

Print answer here A " ☐☐☐☐☐ " ☐☐☐☐

JUMBLE®

Unscramble these four Jumbles, one letter to each square, to form four ordinary words.

HANEY

CUDIL

RUGLAF

NIVIET

Happy 90th birthday!

I've kept things neat and tidy all these years

THE AGED HOUSEKEEPER ATTRIBUTED HER LONGEVITY TO THIS.

Now arrange the circled letters to form the surprise answer, as suggested by the above cartoon.

Print answer here " "

JUMBLE®

Unscramble these four Jumbles, one letter to
each square, to form four ordinary words.

LAGEE

EMARK

LIPPUT

WHYTOR

WHAT THE BUSY
EXECUTIVE
FINISHED OVER
THE WEEKEND.

Now arrange the circled letters to form the
surprise answer, as suggested by the above
cartoon.

*Print
answer
here* HIS " ⬡⬡⬡⬡⬡ " ⬡⬡⬡⬡

JUMBLE®

Unscramble these four Jumbles, one letter to
each square, to form four ordinary words.

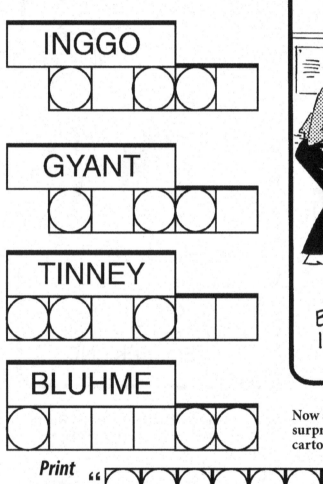

INGGO

GYANT

TINNEY

BLUHME

Hey, it
works

We learned
a lot

BUILDING A LAMP
IN CLASS WAS----

Now arrange the circled letters to form the
surprise answer, as suggested by the above
cartoon.

*Print
answer
here* " ◯◯◯◯◯◯◯◯◯◯◯◯◯ "

JUMBLE®

Unscramble these four Jumbles, one letter to
each square, to form four ordinary words.

NUDAT

ORXAB

FLIDED

LAIVES

Billy needs
a bandage

WHAT THE DOCTOR
CONSIDERED HIS
CHIEF NURSE.

Now arrange the circled letters to form the
surprise answer, as suggested by the above
cartoon.

Print answer here " ⬡⬡⬡⬡⬡ ⬡⬡⬡ "

JUMBLE®

Unscramble these four Jumbles, one letter to
each square, to form four ordinary words.

NORDE

CUSTO

LIVRIE

REDOWP

They'll beat them
by 30 points

You're
crazy.
They
couldn't
beat a
rug

THE KIND OF
ARGUMENT OFTEN
HEARD AT A
SPORTS BAR.

Now arrange the circled letters to form the
surprise answer, as suggested by the above
cartoon.

Print
answer
here

A "◯◯◯◯◯◯◯◯" ◯◯◯

84

JUMBLE®

Unscramble these four Jumbles, one letter to
each square, to form four ordinary words.

SHWIK

NIGVY

ABBIDE

SHUBIL

These artifacts are lovely

What a place

WHAT THE ARCH-
EOLOGIST'S
FRIENDS ADMIRED
WHEN THEY SAW
THE NEW HOUSE.

Now arrange the circled letters to form the
surprise answer, as suggested by the above
cartoon.

Print answer here ⟨◯◯◯⟩ " ◯◯◯◯ "

JUMBLE®

Unscramble these four Jumbles, one letter to
each square, to form four ordinary words.

SWYNE

PAWMS

YARNEL

NITTEY

It's not you, Martha,
it's me

THE PRINTER
BROKE UP WITH
HIS GIRLFRIEND
BECAUSE SHE----

Now arrange the circled letters to form the
surprise answer, as suggested by the above
cartoon.

*Print
answer
here*

⬡⬡⬡⬡ ' ⬡ HIS " ⬡⬡⬡⬡ "

JUMBLE®

Unscramble these four Jumbles, one letter to each square, to form four ordinary words.

TOHRT

YOGUN

LOCCIA

CANUPH

Pipe down. I'm taking a nap

You're it

WHAT DAD TURNED INTO WHEN THE KIDS GOT TOO LOUD.

Now arrange the circled letters to form the surprise answer, as suggested by the above cartoon.

Print answer here

A

JUMBLE®

Unscramble these four Jumbles, one letter to each square, to form four ordinary words.

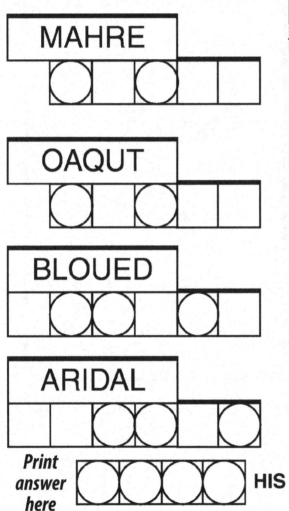

MAHRE

OAQUT

BLOUED

ARIDAL

Print answer here ⬡⬡⬡⬡ **HIS**

Put your fingers around the stem and bottom

THE WINE STEWARD SHOWED THE DINER HOW TO DO THIS.

Now arrange the circled letters to form the surprise answer, as suggested by the above cartoon.

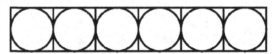

JUMBLE®

Unscramble these four Jumbles, one letter to each square, to form four ordinary words.

VOYIR

RATAL

YERECH

VISWEL

You don't deserve a penny

I'll see you in court

WHAT THE COMBAT PILOTS CONDUCTED WHEN THEIR UNCLE'S WILL WAS READ.

Now arrange the circled letters to form the surprise answer, as suggested by the above cartoon.

Print answer here AN

JUMBLE®

Unscramble these four Jumbles, one letter to each square, to form four ordinary words.

POVER

ROMIN

BOUTID

NORBOC

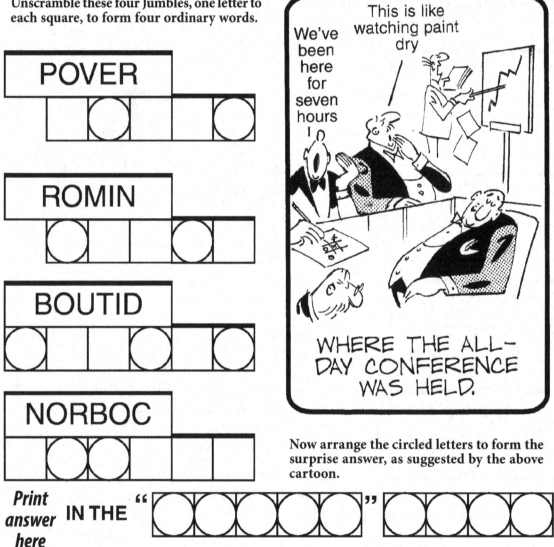

We've been here for seven hours

This is like watching paint dry

WHERE THE ALL-DAY CONFERENCE WAS HELD.

Now arrange the circled letters to form the surprise answer, as suggested by the above cartoon.

Print answer here IN THE " ⬡⬡⬡⬡⬡ " ⬡⬡⬡⬡

JUMBLE®

Unscramble these four Jumbles, one letter to each square, to form four ordinary words.

KIMPS

NADAP

ZELZIF

DREBIG

WHEN HUBBY RAIDED THE COOKIE JAR, THE ASTRONOMER SAID HE WAS----

Now arrange the circled letters to form the surprise answer, as suggested by the above cartoon.

Print answer here THE ⚪⚪⚪ " ⚪⚪⚪⚪⚪⚪ "

JUMBLE®

Unscramble these four Jumbles, one letter to each square, to form four ordinary words.

NARFC

FEACH

YEMINT

PUNACK

I'll be back in two hours

I'll take good care of him

SALOON

WHAT THE COWBOY GOT WHEN HE LEFT HIS HORSE AT THE STABLE.

Now arrange the circled letters to form the surprise answer, as suggested by the above cartoon.

Print answer here

A " ◯◯◯◯ " ◯◯◯◯◯

JUMBLE®

Unscramble these four Jumbles, one letter to each square, to form four ordinary words.

FUINY

OSLOE

ZLIDRA

GIZZAG

Snap to it, Charlie, we're hungry

WHEN HE BARBECUED IN THE HOT SUN, HE WAS----

Now arrange the circled letters to form the surprise answer, as suggested by the above cartoon.

Print answer here " ⬯⬯⬯⬯⬯⬯⬯⬯⬯ "

JUMBLE®

Unscramble these four Jumbles, one letter to
each square, to form four ordinary words.

DEACK

CRATT

RIVFEY

EUGLED

Give it
to the
junkman

It just
needs fixing

WHAT TO DO WITH
AN OLD BROKEN
BIKE.

Now arrange the circled letters to form the
surprise answer, as suggested by the above
cartoon.

Print answer here " ◯◯◯◯◯◯◯ " **IT**

JUMBLE®

Unscramble these four Jumbles, one letter to
each square, to form four ordinary words.

SNUKK

UBLIT

GEDDER

EFFOTE

You said I'd double my money by now

There's been an unforeseen setback

EVICTION NOTICE

WHEN THE FIRE-
MAN FELL FOR
THE SCAM ARTIST'S
PITCH, HE---

Now arrange the circled letters to form the
surprise answer, as suggested by the above
cartoon.

Print answer here

JUMBLE®

Unscramble these four Jumbles, one letter to
each square, to form four ordinary words.

ROBIL

ORGUP

ALVASS

ANNKIP

Oops, I
need a bib

WHAT MOM SAID
WHEN DAD SPILLED
CHOWDER ON
HIS SHIRT.

Now arrange the circled letters to form the
surprise answer, as suggested by the above
cartoon.

Print answer here " ◯◯◯◯ ' ◯ ◯◯ "

JUMBLE®

Unscramble these four Jumbles, one letter to
each square, to form four ordinary words.

GOLIO

BAWLY

CAMEZE

TAGASH

That's your
10th sale
today

I'm gonna
run this place
someday

WHAT THE AMBITIOUS
TIRE SALESMAN
WANTED TO BECOME.

Now arrange the circled letters to form the
surprise answer, as suggested by the above
cartoon.

Print answer here A ◯◯◯ "◯◯◯◯◯◯"

JUMBLE®

Unscramble these four Jumbles, one letter to
each square, to form four ordinary words.

LUXTE

ROWCE

VERROF

THODEB

#%&$&X@ I wasn't
speeding. I'll
have your badge

Come with
me, sir

WHERE THE DRIVER
ENDED UP WHEN
HE GOT HOT UNDER
THE COLLAR.

Now arrange the circled letters to form the
surprise answer, as suggested by the above
cartoon.

Print answer here   IN

JUMBLE®

Unscramble these four Jumbles, one letter to
each square, to form four ordinary words.

MELIP

SOGEO

GUBREO

BLOWEB

This is his
second-favorite
sport

I'm going
for a
perfect game

WHAT THE FOOTBALL
STAR LOOKED
FORWARD TO DURING
THE OFF-SEASON.

Now arrange the circled letters to form the
surprise answer, as suggested by the above
cartoon.

Print
answer
here

A 〇〇〇〇〇 " 〇〇〇〇 "

JUMBLE®

Unscramble these four Jumbles, one letter to
each square, to form four ordinary words.

RATAO

PAKKO

NAHDEL

BUCTAD

That's all the
money I've got

You forgot
the rolls

WHY THE DINER
DIDN'T LEAVE
A TIP.

Now arrange the circled letters to form the
surprise answer, as suggested by the above
cartoon.

*Print
answer
here* HE
WAS ⬡⬡⬡ OF "⬡⬡⬡⬡⬡"

JUMBLE®

Unscramble these four Jumbles, one letter to each square, to form four ordinary words.

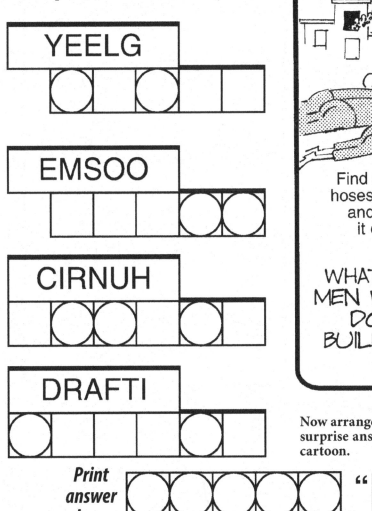

YEELG

EMSOO

CIRNUH

DRAFTI

Find some
hoses, men,
and put
it out

WHAT THE RIFLE-
MEN WERE TOLD TO
DO WHEN THE
BUILDING STARTED
BURNING.

Now arrange the circled letters to form the surprise answer, as suggested by the above cartoon.

Print answer here

"   "

JUMBLE®

Unscramble these four Jumbles, one letter to each square, to form four ordinary words.

HOBOT

YAASS

ALEGEB

GARDIN

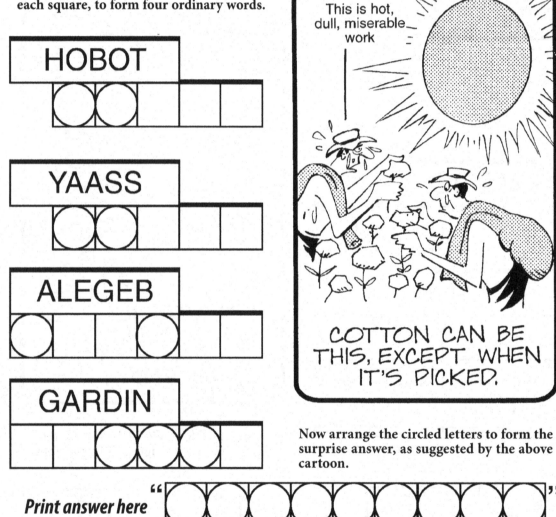

This is hot, dull, miserable work

COTTON CAN BE THIS, EXCEPT WHEN IT'S PICKED.

Now arrange the circled letters to form the surprise answer, as suggested by the above cartoon.

Print answer here "⬡⬡⬡⬡⬡⬡⬡⬡⬡"

JUMBLE®

Unscramble these four Jumbles, one letter to each square, to form four ordinary words.

RYKUM

GOMAD

TRYSAP

ELBARR

I'll have to change all my makeup

Now I can have more fun

WHAT THE BRUNETTES LEFT BEHIND WHEN THEY BECAME BLONDES.

Now arrange the circled letters to form the surprise answer, as suggested by the above cartoon.

Print answer here THE " ⬡⬡⬡⬡ " ⬡⬡⬡⬡

JUMBLE®

Unscramble these four Jumbles, one letter to each square, to form four ordinary words.

DEEKY

CHENE

RALCOR

GAVESA

You won again, sir

$20,000,000

ENJOYED BY THE YOUNG LOTTERY WIN- NER LONG BEFORE HIS TIME.

Now arrange the circled letters to form the surprise answer, as suggested by the above cartoon.

Print answer THE " ☐☐☐☐☐☐ " ☐☐☐☐☐
here

JUMBLE®

Unscramble these four Jumbles, one letter to each square, to form four ordinary words.

TUBIC

FORLO

WALLOH

STEEWF

How 'bout dinner tonight?

Perhaps some other time

WHAT THE PORTRAIT MODEL GAVE THE ARTIST.

Now arrange the circled letters to form the surprise answer, as suggested by the above cartoon.

Print answer here THE "◯◯◯◯◯◯ – ◯◯◯"

JUMBLE®

Unscramble these four Jumbles, one letter to each square, to form four ordinary words.

ALMEY

ELVOG

VERDIF

SPLEET

You'll start at the bottom

But I want to take pictures

WHY THE PHOTO BOSS ASSIGNED THE APPRENTICE TO THE DARKROOM.

Now arrange the circled letters to form the surprise answer, as suggested by the above cartoon.

Print answer here TO " ⌾⌾⌾⌾⌾⌾⌾ "

JUMBLE®

Unscramble these four Jumbles, one letter to
each square, to form four ordinary words.

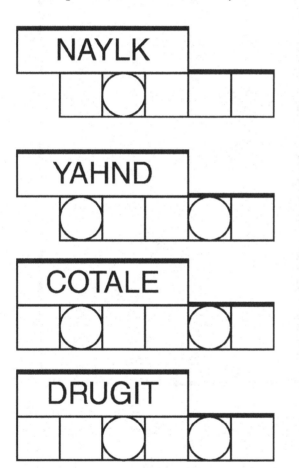

NAYLK

YAHND

COTALE

DRUGIT

Either use that sledge
hammer or take a hike

WHAT THE HIGH-
WAY FOREMAN
WANTED THE LAZY
WORKER TO DO.

Now arrange the circled letters to form the
surprise answer, as suggested by the above
cartoon.

Print answer here " ⃝⃝⃝ " THE ⃝⃝⃝⃝

JUMBLE®

Unscramble these four Jumbles, one letter to each square, to form four ordinary words.

IMECH

SYSUF

GOSTEO

SWILEY

DIET CLASS

Now, promise not to look

GETTING ON A SCALE IN FRONT OF OTHERS CAN BE A----

Now arrange the circled letters to form the surprise answer, as suggested by the above cartoon.

Print answer here " ⬭⬭⬭⬭⬭⬭⬭ " ⬭⬭⬭⬭⬭

JUMBLE®

Unscramble these four Jumbles, one letter to each square, to form four ordinary words.

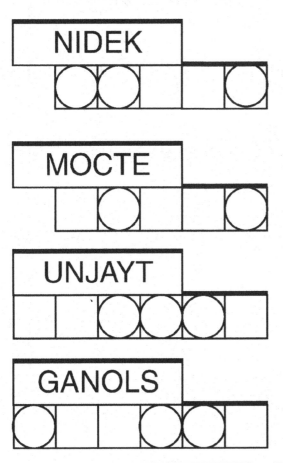

NIDEK

MOCTE

UNJAYT

GANOLS

Take a rest

There's no room, Coach —

WHEN THE SUPERSTAR COULDN'T FIND A SEAT ON THE BENCH, HE WAS----

Now arrange the circled letters to form the surprise answer, as suggested by the above cartoon.

Print answer here ◯◯◯ , ◯◯◯◯◯◯◯◯

JUMBLE®

Unscramble these four Jumbles, one letter to each square, to form four ordinary words.

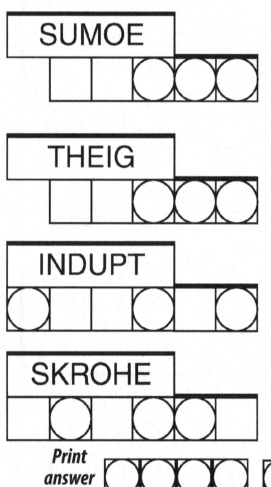

SUMOE

THEIG

INDUPT

SKROHE

Have you read HOMER?

It's about baseball, right?

AVOIDED BY SOMEONE WHO'S SHALLOW-MINDED.

Now arrange the circled letters to form the surprise answer, as suggested by the above cartoon.

Print answer here

JUMBLE®

Unscramble these four Jumbles, one letter to each square, to form four ordinary words.

THAPC

INBAR

UNEEVA

TURUNE

THE EXTERMINATOR QUIT BECAUSE HE WAS TIRED OF THIS.

Now arrange the circled letters to form the surprise answer, as suggested by the above cartoon.

Print answer here **THE** ◯◯◯ ◯◯◯◯◯

JUMBLE®

Unscramble these four Jumbles, one letter to each square, to form four ordinary words.

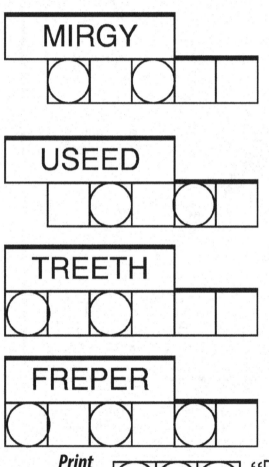

MIRGY

USEED

TREETH

FREPER

I'll be with you shortly, madam

EASY FOR A NECK-WEAR SALESMAN TO DO BEFORE FATHER'S DAY.

Now arrange the circled letters to form the surprise answer, as suggested by the above cartoon.

Print answer here ⬚⬚⬚ "⬚⬚⬚⬚⬚" ⬚⬚

112

JUMBLE®

Unscramble these four Jumbles, one letter to each square, to form four ordinary words.

FLAYE

YOULS

RECRON

THERAH

How 'bout lunch today?

I can't. I've got the wash, the kids, dinner...

A HOMEMAKER IS OFTEN TOO BUSY FOR THIS.

Now arrange the circled letters to form the surprise answer, as suggested by the above cartoon.

Print answer here

JUMBLE®

Unscramble these four Jumbles, one letter to each square, to form four ordinary words.

SHAWS

CATEX

SYNATH

CREHAB

Is there some-thing we have to do?

Just taste and enjoy

TONIGHT ONLY!

ON THE HOUSE

WHEN THE FISH HOUSE OFFERED FREE MEALS, THE COUPLE ASKED---

Now arrange the circled letters to form the surprise answer, as suggested by the above cartoon.

Print answer here

____ ' _ THE " _____ " ?

JUMBLE®

Unscramble these four Jumbles, one letter to each square, to form four ordinary words.

SURBT

HAABS

GINCHA

HARKEW

This will make new plastic, paper, and metal

It'll be worth millions

WHAT THE RECYCLING FIRM GENERATED.

Now arrange the circled letters to form the surprise answer, as suggested by the above cartoon.

Print answer here

JUMBLE®

Unscramble these four Jumbles, one letter to each square, to form four ordinary words.

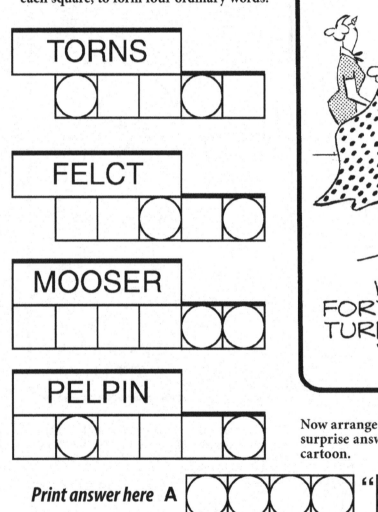

TORNS

FELCT

MOOSER

PELPIN

My hobby is taking photos

WHAT THE FORTUNE-TELLER TURNED INTO ON VACATION.

Now arrange the circled letters to form the surprise answer, as suggested by the above cartoon.

Print answer here **A**  " "

JUMBLE®

Unscramble these four Jumbles, one letter to each square, to form four ordinary words.

REPIK

CAMPH

LICKEF

CISNEC

That's a take

cluck   cluck

peep
peep

WHAT THE DIREC-TOR ENDED UP WITH WHEN HE FILMED THE BARNYARD SCENE.

Now arrange the circled letters to form the surprise answer, as suggested by the above cartoon.

Print answer here A " ☐☐☐☐☐ " ☐☐☐☐☐

JUMBLE®

Unscramble these four Jumbles, one letter to each square, to form four ordinary words.

KEWOA

NOYME

NURULC

TOOWWK

That's his fourth concert in three days

WHAT THE BUSY VIOLINIST WAS UP TO.

Now arrange the circled letters to form the surprise answer, as suggested by the above cartoon.

Print answer here HIS ⬡⬡⬡⬡ IN ⬡⬡⬡⬡

118

JUMBLE®

Unscramble these four Jumbles, one letter to each square, to form four ordinary words.

ZOPAT

DOIMI

GIXNIF

RULSAW

I'll lower taxes and raise income

He's so cute

THE YOUNG CANDI-DATE WAS ELECTED BECAUSE HE WAS----

Now arrange the circled letters to form the surprise answer, as suggested by the above cartoon.

Print answer here " ◯◯◯◯◯◯◯◯◯ "

JUMBLE®

Unscramble these four Jumbles, one letter to each square, to form four ordinary words.

OOCCA

SITOC

BLEETE

VACTOR

I need some aspirin

WHAT THE SALOON KEEPER TOOK WHEN THE COWBOYS GOT ROWDY.

Now arrange the circled letters to form the surprise answer, as suggested by the above cartoon.

Print answer here " ◯◯◯◯◯ "

JUMBLE®

Unscramble these four Jumbles, one letter to each square, to form four ordinary words.

DUIHM

GUAVE

SABBOR

NIGINN

Let's take a break

Want a sandwich?

MOUNTAIN CLIMBERS WILL DO THIS WHILE THEY REST.

Now arrange the circled letters to form the surprise answer, as suggested by the above cartoon.

Print answer here ⭕⭕⭕⭕ ⭕⭕⭕⭕⭕⭕⭕

121

JUMBLE®

Unscramble these four Jumbles, one letter to
each square, to form four ordinary words.

KUFLE

CEMIN

OSANTA

REPHOG

You're leaving
crumbs all over

EATING CHOCOLATE
CHIPS IN BED CAN
CREATE THIS.

Now arrange the circled letters to form the
surprise answer, as suggested by the above
cartoon.

*Print
answer* A
here

" "

JUMBLE®

Unscramble these four Jumbles, one letter to
each square, to form four ordinary words.

SOUDE

SASIB

CRENAK

CHEPSY

He's the symphony's
principal soloist

HIS PIANO
STUDIES LED HIM
TO THE---

Now arrange the circled letters to form the
surprise answer, as suggested by the above
cartoon.

Print
answer
here

" ◯◯◯◯◯ " TO ◯◯◯◯◯◯◯◯

123

JUMBLE®

Unscramble these four Jumbles, one letter to
each square, to form four ordinary words.

DAAMM

KAYWG

ERASHE

KRABEM

Stop hitting me

You started it

STOP THAT!

WHAT DAD FACED
WHEN THE FAMILY
WENT FOR A
DRIVE.

Now arrange the circled letters to form the
surprise answer, as suggested by the above
cartoon.

Print answer here

JUMBLE®

Unscramble these four Jumbles, one letter to each square, to form four ordinary words.

SHOAC

COINT

FRYTAC

KEYRAB

They don't make walls like they used to

WHAT THE COMEDIAN MADE WHEN HIS CAR HIT THE BUILDING.

Now arrange the circled letters to form the surprise answer, as suggested by the above cartoon.

Print answer here

A ⬡⬡⬡⬡⬡ "⬡⬡⬡⬡⬡"

JUMBLE®

Unscramble these four Jumbles, one letter to each square, to form four ordinary words.

RYDYL

LEZBA

IMMORE

FRASIA

Let's ride the big one

WHEN THE TRAIN CONDUCTOR WENT SURFING, IT WAS——

Now arrange the circled letters to form the surprise answer, as suggested by the above cartoon.

Print answer here ☐☐☐ A " ☐☐☐☐☐☐ "

126

JUMBLE®

Unscramble these four Jumbles, one letter to each square, to form four ordinary words.

TAIMY

JAROM

BREHEY

ENLOOD

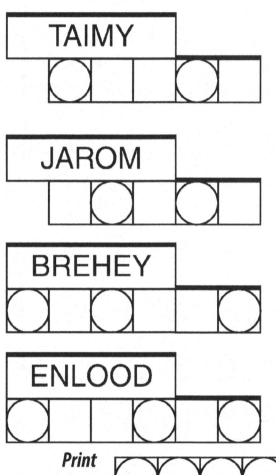

I won't see you for three months

I'll call from college every day

WHAT LAST NIGHT PUT AN END TO.

Now arrange the circled letters to form the surprise answer, as suggested by the above cartoon.

Print answer here

JUMBLE®

Unscramble these four Jumbles, one letter to
each square, to form four ordinary words.

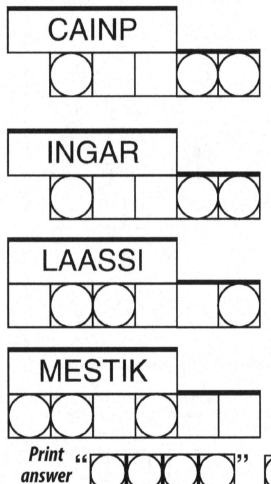

CAINP

INGAR

LAASSI

MESTIK

All I can have
are some vegetables

WHAT SHE FACED
WHEN SHE STARTED
HER DIET.

Now arrange the circled letters to form the
surprise answer, as suggested by the above
cartoon.

*Print
answer
here* " ⬭⬭⬭⬭ " ⬭⬭⬭⬭⬭⬭⬭⬭⬭

JUMBLE®

Unscramble these four Jumbles, one letter to
each square, to form four ordinary words.

EVVAL

LOVEH

RAXLYN

BALIVE

This job is out
of this world

HOW THE PLANET-
ARIUM WORKER
DESCRIBED HIS
WORK.

Now arrange the circled letters to form the
surprise answer, as suggested by the above
cartoon.

Print answer here " ◯◯◯◯◯◯◯◯ "

JUMBLE®

Unscramble these four Jumbles, one letter to each square, to form four ordinary words.

ARVEG

CALVO

ASHRIP

TIFLLE

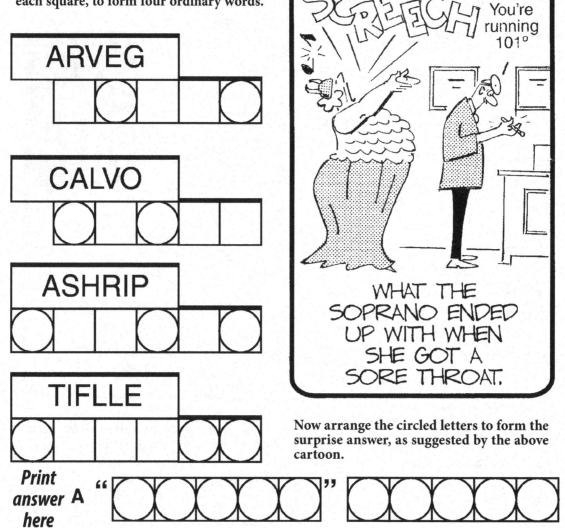

SCREECH You're running 101°

WHAT THE SOPRANO ENDED UP WITH WHEN SHE GOT A SORE THROAT.

Now arrange the circled letters to form the surprise answer, as suggested by the above cartoon.

Print answer here " ◯◯◯◯◯ " ◯◯◯◯◯

JUMBLE®

Unscramble these four Jumbles, one letter to
each square, to form four ordinary words.

MARDA

REDOO

MENECT

HERNID

Put on
some sun
lotion

Ah, this
is the
life

WHAT THE
LEATHER-MAKER
DID ON VACATION.

Now arrange the circled letters to form the
surprise answer, as suggested by the above
cartoon.

Print "⬡⬡⬡⬡⬡⬡⬡" **HIS** ⬡⬡⬡⬡
*answer
here*

JUMBLE®

Unscramble these four Jumbles, one letter to
each square, to form four ordinary words.

NOOZE

SERCS

TAUMUN

FLERBY

The lookouts
fell asleep

They're
busted

WHAT THE SAILORS
ENDED UP WITH
WHEN THE SHIP
RAN AGROUND.

Now arrange the circled letters to form the
surprise answer, as suggested by the above
cartoon.

*Print
answer
here*

A ☐☐☐ OF ☐☐☐☐☐☐☐

JUMBLE®

Unscramble these four Jumbles, one letter to each square, to form four ordinary words.

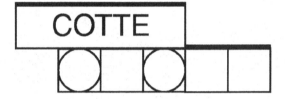

COTTE

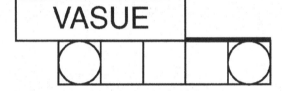

VASUE

CRAFTO

LAMDAY

They come in blue, red, and brown

I'll take 'em all

50% OFF

WHY SHE SPLURGED ON THE SHOES.

Now arrange the circled letters to form the surprise answer, as suggested by the above cartoon.

Print answer here

A ⬡⬡⬡⬡ WAS ⬡⬡⬡⬡⬡

JUMBLE®

Unscramble these four Jumbles, one letter to
each square, to form four ordinary words.

HICCK

MAULB

REENOC

ERWANS

Pull over!

P.D.

WHAT HE ENDED
UP WITH WHEN HE
DROVE AFTER
SOME DRINKS.

Now arrange the circled letters to form the
surprise answer, as suggested by the above
cartoon.

Print answer here **A** " ◯◯◯◯◯◯ "

JUMBLE®

Unscramble these four Jumbles, one letter to each square, to form four ordinary words.

POUCE

PIDEB

JASTUD

BARJEB

Only 36 easy payments of $400 a month

I can't make up my mind

SAL

BUYING A NEW CAR LEFT HIM----

Now arrange the circled letters to form the surprise answer, as suggested by the above cartoon.

Print answer here

TO " "

JUMBLE®

Unscramble these four Jumbles, one letter to each square, to form four ordinary words.

RAWEY

YARPT

REVABE

LAMDET

I do all my research here

WHY THE SEER VISITED THE LIBRARY.

Now arrange the circled letters to form the surprise answer, as suggested by the above cartoon.

Print answer here   TO   "〇〇〇〇"   〇〇〇〇〇〇〇

JUMBLE®

Unscramble these four Jumbles, one letter to each square, to form four ordinary words.

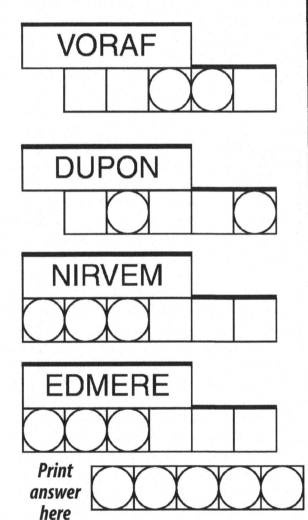

VORAF

DUPON

NIRVEM

EDMERE

Yee haw   Git along now

WHAT THE COW-
BOYS DID WITH
THE HERD OF
CATTLE.

Now arrange the circled letters to form the surprise answer, as suggested by the above cartoon.

Print answer here ⬡⬡⬡⬡⬡ **THE** ⬡⬡⬡⬡⬡

JUMBLE®

Unscramble these four Jumbles, one letter to each square, to form four ordinary words.

ZAHLE

TENKO

WHARRO

DRYWAT

— That's it. I quit!

I think I'd like a window here

WHAT THE BRICK-LAYER DID WHEN SHE CHANGED HER MIND.

Now arrange the circled letters to form the surprise answer, as suggested by the above cartoon.

Print answer here ⬡⬡⬡⬡⬡ **IN THE** ⬡⬡⬡⬡⬡⬡

JUMBLE®

Unscramble these four Jumbles, one letter to
each square, to form four ordinary words.

DUXEE

JOUMB

PYRSOD

KAUMPE

Nice
beat

WHEN BUSINESS
WENT DOWN AT
THE MUSIC
STORE, HE---

Now arrange the circled letters to form the
surprise answer, as suggested by the above
cartoon.

*Print answer
here* " ☐☐☐☐☐☐☐ " **IT** ☐☐

JUMBLE®

Unscramble these four Jumbles, one letter to
each square, to form four ordinary words.

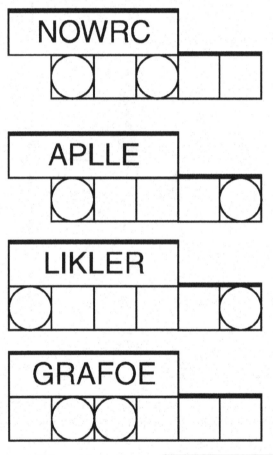

NOWRC

APLLE

LIKLER

GRAFOE

WHAT THE MUSICIANS
EXPERIENCED
IN THE STORMY
SEA.

Now arrange the circled letters to form the
surprise answer, as suggested by the above
cartoon.

Print answer here ⬜ AND ⬜

140

JUMBLE®

Unscramble these four Jumbles, one letter to each square, to form four ordinary words.

ORRIP

BYLUR

DEECCA

BAMLOG

Can't sell a thing lately

WHEN THE STRUG-GLING ARTIST DIDN'T SELL HIS WORK, HE SAID IT WAS---

Now arrange the circled letters to form the surprise answer, as suggested by the above cartoon.

Print answer HIS " ◯◯◯◯ " ◯◯◯◯◯◯ *here*

JUMBLE®

Unscramble these four Jumbles, one letter to
each square, to form four ordinary words.

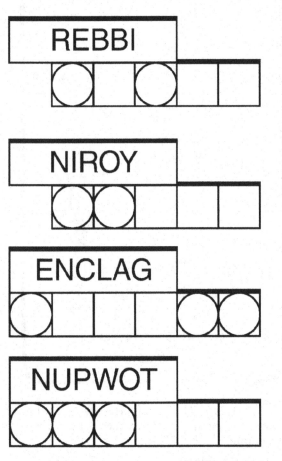

REBBI

NIROY

ENCLAG

NUPWOT

All things considered,
this is the best deal

WHAT THE DEEP
THINKER FOCUSED
ON WHEN HE
BOUGHT A LARGE-
SCREEN TV.

Now arrange the circled letters to form the
surprise answer, as suggested by the above
cartoon.

Print answer   THE "◯◯◯ ◯◯◯◯◯◯◯"
here

JUMBLE

Unscramble these four Jumbles, one letter to
each square, to form four ordinary words.

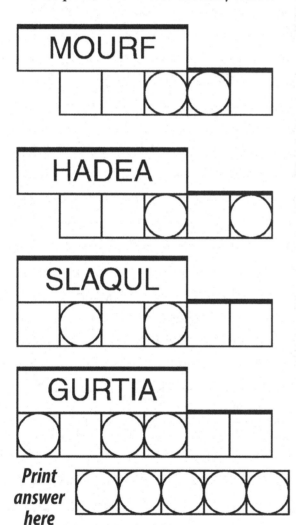

MOURF

HADEA

SLAQUL

GURTIA

It takes forever
to get ready

WHEN THE FEMALE
IMPERSONATOR
PREPARED FOR THE
SHOW, IT WAS----

Now arrange the circled letters to form the
surprise answer, as suggested by the above
cartoon.

Print
answer
here

A " "

JUMBLE®

Unscramble these four Jumbles, one letter to each square, to form four ordinary words.

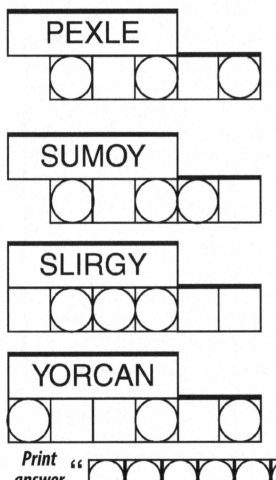

PEXLE

SUMOY

SLIRGY

YORCAN

Have you seen the tuition bill?

That's more than your clothing allowance

WHAT IT COST THE KING TO EDUCATE HIS SONS.

Now arrange the circled letters to form the surprise answer, as suggested by the above cartoon.

Print answer here "⟨◯◯◯◯◯◯◯◯◯⟩" ⟨◯◯◯◯⟩

JUMBLE®

Unscramble these four Jumbles, one letter to each square, to form four ordinary words.

NACHT

TYFFI

YARREP

ENCOBA

WHERE THE TREE TRIMMER APPLIED FOR THE BANK LOAN.

Now arrange the circled letters to form the surprise answer, as suggested by the above cartoon.

Print answer here THE " ⬭⬭⬭⬭⬭⬭ " ⬭⬭⬭⬭⬭⬭

JUMBLE®

Unscramble these four Jumbles, one letter to each square, to form four ordinary words.

BARRI

ENGOM

LALCOW

BONKER

WHAT THE KIDS TURNED THE DEN INTO ON A RAINY DAY.

Now arrange the circled letters to form the surprise answer, as suggested by the above cartoon.

Print answer A "⬚⬚⬚⬚⬚⬚" ⬚⬚⬚⬚
here

JUMBLE®

Unscramble these four Jumbles, one letter to
each square, to form four ordinary words.

UGLIE

PAUNC

SHULOC

RETIGO

Love ya, darlin', be
home in a bit

WHEN THE UMP
DIALED HIS WIFE
ON THEIR ANNI-
VERSARY, HE MADE——

Now arrange the circled letters to form the
surprise answer, as suggested by the above
cartoon.

*Print
answer
here*   THE ⬡⬡⬡⬡⬡ "⬡⬡⬡⬡"

JUMBLE®

Unscramble these four Jumbles, one letter to
each square, to form four ordinary words.

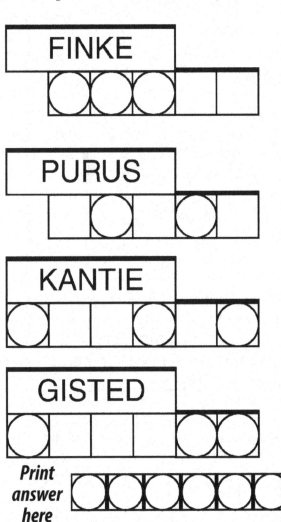

FINKE

PURUS

KANTIE

GISTED

Get out of my room! MOM!

Yecchh!

WHAT SIS DID
WHEN JUNIOR
PLAYED WITH
HER PERFUME.

Now arrange the circled letters to form the
surprise answer, as suggested by the above
cartoon.

Print
answer
here

A " "

JUMBLE®

Unscramble these four Jumbles, one letter to
each square, to form four ordinary words.

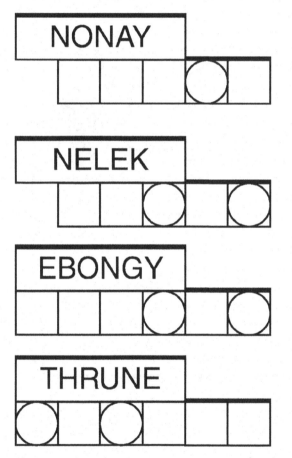

NONAY

NELEK

EBONGY

THRUNE

I need a
new pair

WHAT DAD ENDED
UP WITH WHEN HE
PUT ON HIS
GOLF SOCKS.

Now arrange the circled letters to form the
surprise answer, as suggested by the above
cartoon.

Print answer here **A** " ⬭⬭⬭⬭ **IN** ⬭⬭⬭ "

JUMBLE®

Unscramble these four Jumbles, one letter to each square, to form four ordinary words.

KLANB

LUFTO

LUSSTY

SHOIBY

I feel awful. Must be coming down with something

This will fix you right up

WHAT THE BAR-TENDER OFFERED THE ACHY, FEVER-ISH CUSTOMER.

Now arrange the circled letters to form the surprise answer, as suggested by the above cartoon.

Print answer here **A** ⬡⬡⬡ " ⬡⬡⬡⬡ "

JUMBLE®

Unscramble these four Jumbles, one letter to
each square, to form four ordinary words.

IMMAX

JARAH

TENNIV

TRALFE

!'ll have a sandwich
and a salad

That'll
be $10.00

NO LONGER
INCLUDED IN THE
AIRFARE.

Now arrange the circled letters to form the
surprise answer, as suggested by the above
cartoon.

Print answer here **THE** ◯◯◯ " ◯◯◯◯ "

JUMBLE®

Unscramble these four Jumbles, one letter to
each square, to form four ordinary words.

HAFFC

EXVIN

DIPALL

TRAULB

What
caused
this?

We're
digging
out the
facts

WHAT THE
SCIENTIST WANTED
TO DO AFTER THE
EARTHQUAKE.

Now arrange the circled letters to form the
surprise answer, as suggested by the above
cartoon.

*Print
answer
here*

" "

JUMBLE®

Unscramble these four Jumbles, one letter to
each square, to form four ordinary words.

VAHNE

PLYSH

CLEBUK

TURAIN

Now erase it and
return to your seat

I will not talk in c
not talk in class. I
will not talk in cla
I will not talk in
will talk in cla
I will talk in cla

WHEN THE PUPIL
COMPLETED HIS
PUNISHMENT, HE
ENDED UP WITH----

Now arrange the circled letters to form the
surprise answer, as suggested by the above
cartoon.

*Print
answer
here* A 〇〇〇〇〇 " 〇〇〇〇〇 "

JUMBLE®

Unscramble these four Jumbles, one letter to
each square, to form four ordinary words.

SILAA

DOLMY

BEPSIC

LIMBEN

WHAT HAPPENED
WHEN THE STORE
REDUCED THE
PRICE OF LADDERS.

Now arrange the circled letters to form the
surprise answer, as suggested by the above
cartoon.

**Print
answer
here**

"   "

JUMBLE®

Unscramble these four Jumbles, one letter to
each square, to form four ordinary words.

NIGTY

GUFED

ROESIE

TARRMY

We'll make this
community safe

WHEN THE POLICE
CHIEF ANNOUNCED
HIS CRIME CRACK-
DOWN, HIS REMARKS
WERE---

Now arrange the circled letters to form the
surprise answer, as suggested by the above
cartoon.

*Print
answer
here*

" ◯◯◯◯◯◯◯◯◯◯ "

JUMBLE®

Unscramble these four Jumbles, one letter to each square, to form four ordinary words.

FLATA

LUCCK

CRIONI

KALLIA

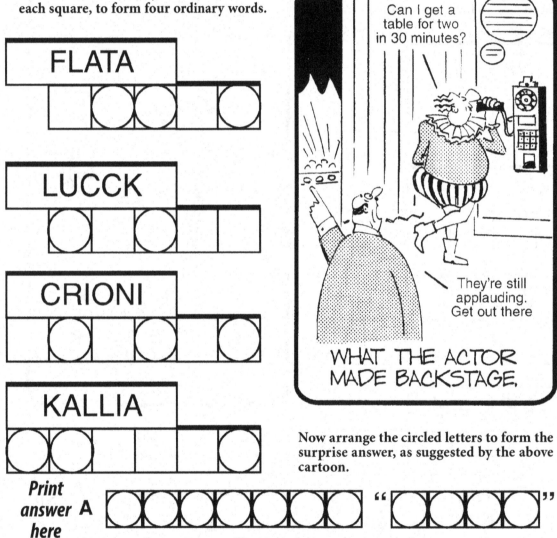

Can I get a table for two in 30 minutes?

They're still applauding. Get out there

WHAT THE ACTOR MADE BACKSTAGE.

Now arrange the circled letters to form the surprise answer, as suggested by the above cartoon.

Print answer here A ⃝⃝⃝⃝⃝⃝⃝ " ⃝⃝⃝⃝ "

JUMBLE®

Unscramble these four Jumbles, one letter to
each square, to form four ordinary words.

LISKY

HECEK

TAJECK

UNPIRT

APPROVED

Our rate
is 5%, not
2%. You
never learn

WHY THE BANKER
FIRED THE LOAN
OFFICER.

Now arrange the circled letters to form the
surprise answer, as suggested by the above
cartoon.

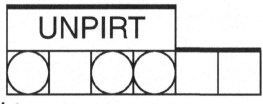

Print
answer
here

 OF ""

157

JUMBLE®

Unscramble these four Jumbles, one letter to
each square, to form four ordinary words.

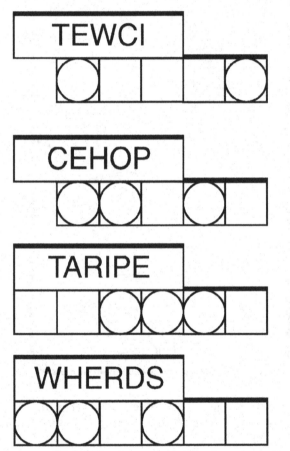

TEWCI

CEHOP

TARIPE

WHERDS

Rover barks one for
red and twice for green

He's
well
trained

WHAT THE CLASS
CONSIDERED THE
DRIVING INSTRUC-
TOR'S DOG.

Now arrange the circled letters to form the
surprise answer, as suggested by the above
cartoon.

*Print
answer
here*

◯◯◯◯◯◯ ' ◯ " ◯◯◯ "

JUMBLE®

Unscramble these four Jumbles, one letter to
each square, to form four ordinary words.

VOCEL

ENPOY

AXROTH

CIVONE

It's all framed and
ready for pouring

NEEDED BEFORE
THE CEMENT
TRUCK ARRIVES.

Now arrange the circled letters to form the
surprise answer, as suggested by the above
cartoon.

Print
answer
here

A " ☐☐☐☐☐☐☐☐ " ☐☐☐☐

JUMBLE®

Unscramble these four Jumbles, one letter to each square, to form four ordinary words.

MILTI

YASOP

INTOOM

EMBACE

I love your outfit

She caught a whopper

WHAT SHE WAS FISHING FOR ON VACATION.

Now arrange the circled letters to form the surprise answer, as suggested by the above cartoon.

Print answer here "☐☐☐☐☐☐☐☐☐☐☐☐☐"

JUMBLE®

Unscramble these four Jumbles, one letter to each square, to form four ordinary words.

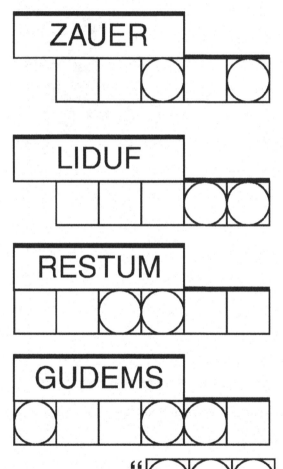

ZAUER

LIDUF

RESTUM

GUDEMS

I just bought it last week

HOW HE FELT WHEN A SUDDEN WIND BLEW A TREE DOWN ON HIS CAR.

Now arrange the circled letters to form the surprise answer, as suggested by the above cartoon.

Print answer here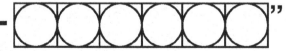

JUMBLE.

Unscramble these four Jumbles, one letter to each square, to form four ordinary words.

MAROA

ORPEN

BRUMEN

MEBBUN

There goes my early tee time

That means you can help around the house all day

WHAT A GOLFER WILL DO ON A RAINY SATURDAY.

Now arrange the circled letters to form the surprise answer, as suggested by the above cartoon.

Print answer here ⬡⬡⬡⬡⬡ THE ⬡⬡⬡⬡

JUMBLE®

Jambalaya

Challenger Puzzles

JUMBLE®

Unscramble these six Jumbles, one letter to
each square, to form six ordinary words.

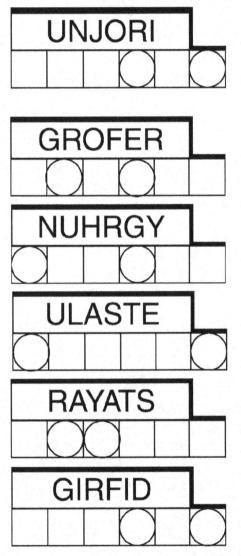

UNJORI

GROFER

NUHRGY

ULASTE

RAYATS

GIRFID

I can't get enough of this vista

I need more film

WHAT THEY DID
WHEN THEY VISITED
THE GRAND CANYON.

Now arrange the circled letters to form the
surprise answer, as suggested by the above
cartoon.

Print answer here

" ⬡⬡⬡⬡⬡⬡ " ON THE ⬡⬡⬡⬡⬡⬡

JUMBLE®

Unscramble these six Jumbles, one letter to each square, to form six ordinary words.

DINNAL

BABFLY

DEWLOP

LUBOSE

RICKYT

PANNEM

Dear, do I put them in whole, or do I grind them?

JUST MARRIED

SHE COULDN'T MAKE A GOOD CUP OF COFFEE BECAUSE SHE---

Now arrange the circled letters to form the surprise answer, as suggested by the above cartoon.

Print answer here

165

JUMBLE.

Unscramble these six Jumbles, one letter to each square, to form six ordinary words.

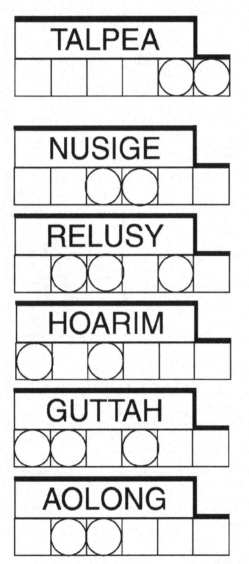

TALPEA

NUSIGE

RELUSY

HOARIM

GUTTAH

AOLONG

...and when the minister sneezed, he said, "Bless you"— get it?

You're fired

WHEN THE JOKE BOMBED, THE THEATER MANAGER SAID IT WAS NO----

Now arrange the circled letters to form the surprise answer, as suggested by the above cartoon.

Print answer here

JUMBLE®

Unscramble these six Jumbles, one letter to
each square, to form six ordinary words.

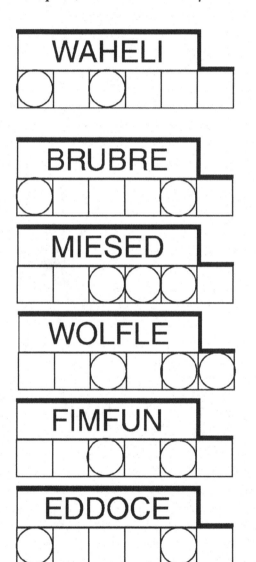

WAHELI

BRUBRE

MIESED

WOLFLE

FIMFUN

EDDOCE

WHEN HE FLUNKED
THE VOCABULARY
TEST ---

Now arrange the circled letters to form the
surprise answer, as suggested by the above
cartoon.

Print answer here

JUMBLE®

Unscramble these six Jumbles, one letter to
each square, to form six ordinary words.

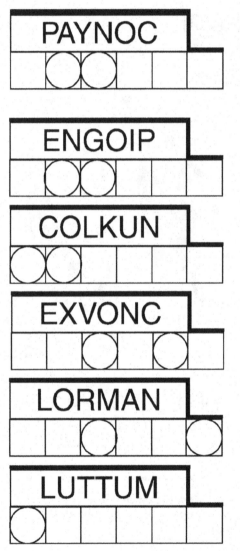

PAYNOC

ENGOIP

COLKUN

EXVONC

LORMAN

LUTTUM

Stop, I
got caught
in traffic

WHY THE TRACK
STAR MISSED
HIS FLIGHT.

Now arrange the circled letters to form the
surprise answer, as suggested by the above
cartoon.

Print answer here

HE WAS " ⬡⬡⬡⬡⬡⬡⬡ " ⬡⬡⬡⬡

JUMBLE®

Unscramble these six Jumbles, one letter to
each square, to form six ordinary words.

ANNOYC

GYSSAR

TIDOAR

SEELAW

DIBITT

YIVELT

Another
round
on me

...that old
gang o' mine

A BUNCH OF BEER
BELLIES CAN TURN
A BAR INTO THIS.

Now arrange the circled letters to form the
surprise answer, as suggested by the above
cartoon.

Print answer here

A "" - ""

JUMBLE®

Unscramble these six Jumbles, one letter to each square, to form six ordinary words.

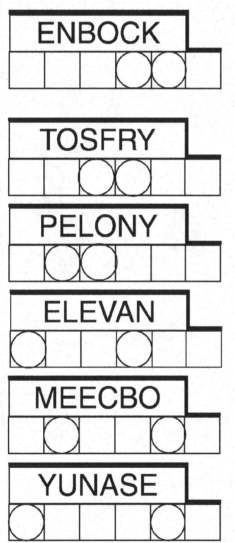

ENBOCK

TOSFRY

PELONY

ELEVAN

MEECBO

YUNASE

Nonstop for over three hours

But very profound

WHAT THE FAMOUS AUTHOR DID WHEN HE GAVE A LECTURE.

Now arrange the circled letters to form the surprise answer, as suggested by the above cartoon.

Print answer here

HE ⬡⬡⬡⬡⬡ "⬡⬡⬡⬡⬡⬡⬡"

JUMBLE

Unscramble these six Jumbles, one letter to each square, to form six ordinary words.

WECHEN

CHELIN

IMLISE

ECHTIC

LESTUS

THOGTE

Make sure the address is prominent

WHAT THE EYE DOCTOR WANTED HIS NEW LOCATION AD TO DO.

Now arrange the circled letters to form the surprise answer, as suggested by the above cartoon.

Print answer here

JUMBLE®

Unscramble these six Jumbles, one letter to
each square, to form six ordinary words.

DIMYAD

WAIRND

EXPLUD

SCOFIA

WODASH

GLOBEN

THE TATTOO ARTIST
GOT THE JOB
BECAUSE HE MADE----

Now arrange the circled letters to form the
surprise answer, as suggested by the above
cartoon.

Print answer here

A

JUMBLE®

Unscramble these six Jumbles, one letter to
each square, to form six ordinary words.

TREOTT

GONEXY

FOUTTI

RILLAP

EXFRIP

VISTEN

$16,000 a month
alimony and she
gets the house

WHAT THE LEADING
MAN GOT WHEN HE
WAS DIVORCED.

Now arrange the circled letters to form the
surprise answer, as suggested by the above
cartoon.

Print answer here

A " ◯◯◯◯◯◯◯◯◯◯◯ " ◯◯◯◯

JUMBLE®

Unscramble these six Jumbles, one letter to
each square, to form six ordinary words.

CATLEK

DORRIT

TOBLET

RITHEE

CLUDGE

LEEXAH

HEARD AT A BUS
STOP ON A COLD,
SNOWY NIGHT.

Now arrange the circled letters to form the
surprise answer, as suggested by the above
cartoon.

Print answer here

174

JUMBLE®

Unscramble these six Jumbles, one letter to each square, to form six ordinary words.

UNRATT

INBOUN

RAMPUK

TARGEY

DOGAPA

VOORDE

WHAT THE CLASS DID WHEN THEY VISITED THE PRIMATE HOUSE.

Now arrange the circled letters to form the surprise answer, as suggested by the above cartoon.

Print answer here

JUMBLE®

Unscramble these six Jumbles, one letter to
each square, to form six ordinary words.

ALFACI

IMDOYF

TRACCI

EXLANF

EUMMUS

LARPOR

WHEE!

I haven't been on this since I was your age

WHEN HE RODE
THE MERRY-GO-
ROUND WITH HIS
SON, DAD SAID
HE HAD----

Now arrange the circled letters to form the
surprise answer, as suggested by the above
cartoon.

Print answer here

JUMBLE®

Unscramble these six Jumbles, one letter to
each square, to form six ordinary words.

PABURT

FALOFY

NIROPS

ORMOAN

CROGED

SIBOPH

No! No! Take the 483 to Route 4. You'll save an hour

He graduated with honors in England

THE YOUNG TRUCKER DEPENDED ON THE DISPATCHER BECAUSE HE WAS----

Now arrange the circled letters to form the surprise answer, as suggested by the above cartoon.

Print answer here

A " ☐☐☐☐☐ " ☐☐☐☐☐☐☐

177

JUMBLE®

Unscramble these six Jumbles, one letter to each square, to form six ordinary words.

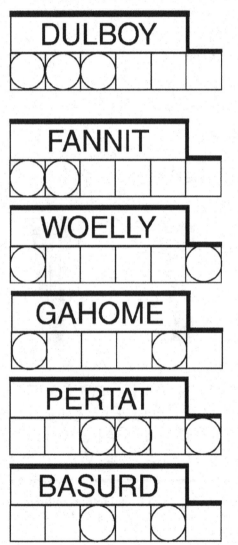

DULBOY

FANNIT

WOELLY

GAHOME

PERTAT

BASURD

I should double my money in two years

THE MOGUL INVESTED IN THE NURSERY BECAUSE IT WAS A----

Now arrange the circled letters to form the surprise answer, as suggested by the above cartoon.

Print answer here

178

JUMBLE®

Unscramble these six Jumbles, one letter to each square, to form six ordinary words.

LUNFIX

PYTSHU

TIQUEY

RANCOB

KUPHOO

GILOOG

I can hardly move my arms

Is that my yarn or yours?

WHEN THE CROCHET CLASS MET IN A SMALLER ROOM, THEY BECAME A----

Now arrange the circled letters to form the surprise answer, as suggested by the above cartoon.

Print answer here

◯◯◯◯◯ - ◯◯◯◯◯ ◯◯◯◯◯

JUMBLE®

Unscramble these six Jumbles, one letter to each square, to form six ordinary words.

REYGES

STINCH

CHOROT

CILIAT

NOOPUC

UNRATE

Tickets

Ten more pages of philosophy, and then I can take a nap

THE STUDENT TURNED HIS RAIL RIDE INTO A----

Now arrange the circled letters to form the surprise answer, as suggested by the above cartoon.

Print answer here

" ◯◯◯◯◯ " OF ◯◯◯◯◯◯◯

JUMBLE.

Unscramble these six Jumbles, one letter to each square, to form six ordinary words.

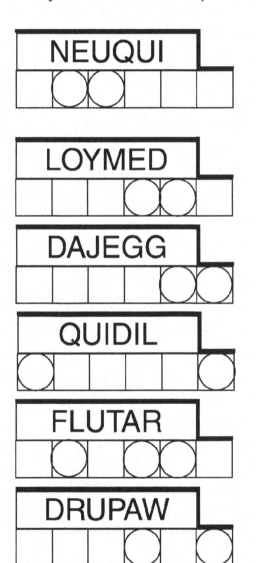

NEUQUI

LOYMED

DAJEGG

QUIDIL

FLUTAR

DRUPAW

En garde

Sit down and pay attention

THE PROFESSOR SCOLDED THE VIOLIN STUDENTS BECAUSE THEY----

Now arrange the circled letters to form the surprise answer, as suggested by the above cartoon.

Print answer here

" ◯◯◯◯◯◯◯ " ◯◯◯◯◯◯

JUMBLE®

Unscramble these six Jumbles, one letter to
each square, to form six ordinary words.

ASHIMP

POMCLE

ODRANG

FUELEY

FLEEBI

CURPES

She's a
doll

And very
smart

WHAT THE BEAUTY
QUEEN TURNED
INTO WHEN SHE
ADDRESSED THE
CROWD.

Now arrange the circled letters to form the
surprise answer, as suggested by the above
cartoon.

Print answer here

A " ⬡⬡⬡⬡⬡⬡ " OF ⬡⬡⬡⬡⬡⬡

JUMBLE®

Unscramble these six Jumbles, one letter to each square, to form six ordinary words.

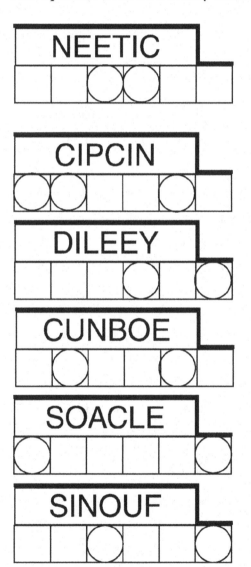

NEETIC

CIPCIN

DILEEY

CUNBOE

SOACLE

SINOUF

She gets the house and cars. You get the bills

THE DIVORCE JUDGE GAVE THE BOXER A----

Now arrange the circled letters to form the surprise answer, as suggested by the above cartoon.

Print answer here

" ◯◯◯◯◯ " ◯◯◯◯◯◯◯◯◯

Answers

1. **Jumbles** DADDY LAPEL CANKER CROTCH
   Answer: Back then, when the auto wouldn't start, the driver became—"CRANKY"

2. **Jumbles** FLOUT TONIC PIRATE MUSTER
   Answer: Nobody knew the spy wore a toupee because it was—"TOP" SECRET

3. **Jumbles** LUCID SYLPH FEUDAL PEWTER
   Answer: When he promised this, the tailor running for office—"SEWED" IT UP

4. **Jumbles** DRYLY AWOKE ARMADA MOTION
   Answer: What he had on when he was awakened—A RADIO

5. **Jumbles** GUARD TRACT CHUBBY ACHING
   Answer: When Dad arrived in time to see his son's spectacular play, he—"CAUGHT" THE CATCH

6. **Jumbles** GULCH PRIOR NEARBY FEMALE
   Answer: When he got engaged, he became—A BELLE "RINGER"

7. **Jumbles** MINCE AHEAD GUTTER HAPPEN
   Answer: The manager said the winning southpaw was his—RIGHT-HAND MAN

8. **Jumbles** BULLY PRONE BEYOND BUCKET
   Answer: When the juggler kept dropping the ball, he was—"BOUNCED"

9. **Jumbles** WHOSE NAVAL BANANA IMPOSE
   Answer: What she hoped her mother would get when her new beau came calling—A SON-IN-LAW

10. **Jumbles** TOKEN GOURD SCRIBE BOYISH
    Answer: How the repair shop made money selling laces—ON A SHOESTRING

11. **Jumbles** LIMIT DUMPY HAUNCH JANGLE
    Answer: What the female detectives conducted at the singles bar—A MANHUNT

12. **Jumbles** CRAWL JADED COBALT CALMLY
    Answer: When Junior didn't wash the windows, Mom was—"CLEARLY" MAD

13. **Jumbles** FLUID POKER PUDDLE DEADLY
    Answer: What the greyhound did during the race—"LAPPED" THE FIELD

14. **Jumbles** ALIAS KNEEL BURIAL POPLAR
    Answer: Easy for pig farmers to grow—PORK BELLIES

15. **Jumbles** POUCH CREEL POTTER TAWDRY
    Answer: How they felt when they took a trip down under—ON TOP OF THE WORLD

16. **Jumbles** DICED NIPPY THORAX PRIMER
    Answer: The medical student's favorite section in the textbook—THE APPENDIX

17. **Jumbles** TROTH FUDGE GLOBAL POETRY
    Answer: Why he started studying insects—HE GOT THE BUG

18. **Jumbles** MOLDY HENNA ABOUND BRUTAL
    Answer: After a few drinks, the hunter and his rifle were—BOTH LOADED

19. **Jumbles** CROON POPPY UPKEEP MEMBER
    Answer: When he got the bill for her new glasses, it was—AN EYE-OPENER

20. **Jumbles** MAUVE PIANO HOTBED WINNOW
    Answer: What Dad needed after sitting at the computer for hours—"DOWN" TIME

21. **Jumbles** SOAPY GAVEL DISMAL JACKET
    Answer: Why the quarterback was a lousy bridge player—HE LIKED TO "PASS"

22. **Jumbles** STAID GLORY GLANCE INDUCE
    Answer: When the best man made a toast, he was—"SINGLED" OUT

23. **Jumbles** CRANK ARBOR STYMIE CAVORT
    Answer: What the new sailor had on his first voyage—A "ROCK-Y" START

24. **Jumbles** TWICE IRONY DETAIN SLUICE
    Answer: What the marriage counselor gave the troubled couple—A "WED-UCATION"

25. **Jumbles** EPOCH SILKY JUNGLE BOUNTY
    Answer: When the brawler bought a pre-owned car, the salesman said he was—A "TOUGH" SELL

26. **Jumbles** DRAWL BELLE UPTOWN TINKLE
    Answer: Often heard in a bedding store—PILLOW TALK

27. **Jumbles** OPIUM JUICE NEGATE LIMBER
    Answer: What the muralist focused on when he completed his work—THE BIG PICTURE

28. **Jumbles** TYING GLAND THROAT INNING
    Answer: A beautiful sunset makes a difference in this—DAY AND NIGHT

29. **Jumbles** KNIFE QUOTA JACKAL PARODY
    Answer: What the dog catcher got on his birthday—"POUND" CAKE

30. **Jumbles** BALKY MOTIF HARROW VERMIN
    Answer: Sold in butcher shops but seldom served in restaurants—RAW MEAT

31. **Jumbles** FIFTY NIECE RITUAL VERSUS
    Answer: Twenty-four hours on shore gave the sailors this—A "FLEET" VISIT

32. **Jumbles** FELON AGENT GYPSUM KIMONO
    Answer: What he turned into when the exotic birds were stolen—A STOOL PIGEON

33. **Jumbles** EIGHT DOUSE CARPET DRUDGE
    Answer: When Rover finished obedience school, he had a—"PET-DEGREE"

34. **Jumbles** INKED FORGO HOOKED SEPTIC
    Answer: It often takes this to put up with bad manners—GOOD ONES

35. **Jumbles** QUILT SHOWY ATTAIN PALACE
    Answer: When the quick tire change was botched, the racer said his loss was—THE "PITS"

36. **Jumbles** COLIC ABATE SHAKEN TEAPOT
    Answer: What Dad did while watching the pet show—TOOK A CATNAP

37. **Jumbles** BASIN PERKY DOMINO JOSTLE
    Answer: When the comedian failed to appear, the nightclub owner said—"IT'S NO JOKE"

38. **Jumbles** CROUP FUSSY POROUS PURPLE
    Answer: Why the reporter visited the ice-cream parlor—FOR A "SCOOP"

39. **Jumbles** TAWNY VENOM GAINED WISELY
    Answer: When the elevator got stuck on the way up, the riders said—IT WAS "DOWN"

40. **Jumbles** CHAOS CRESS FORCED IMPUGN
    Answer: What she "weighed" before starting her diet—THE PROS AND CONS

41. **Jumbles** SHAKY ABYSS HOMING NEPHEW
    Answer: The quarterback pursuing the cheerleader was noted for—MAKING "PASSES"

42. **Jumbles** FATAL ABOVE FORGOT TALKER
    Answer: What the nervous flyer wanted to do as departure time neared—TAKE OFF

43. **Jumbles** MIDGE CHANT ACTUAL PLEDGE
    Answer: Good advice for an obsessive dieter—"LIGHTEN" UP

44. **Jumbles** MINER CURRY MEDLEY ROTATE
    Answer: What the tour golfer–turned-butcher did—MADE THE "CUT"

45. **Jumbles** SUAVE PRIZE ZODIAC CLOTHE
    Answer: What they faced when they studied for final exams—SCHOOL "DAZE"

46. **Jumbles** PECAN FRAME HEREBY OUTWIT
    Answer: What the professor considered the student's solution to the equation—A "MATH-TERPIECE"

47. **Jumbles** ERASE LURID GUZZLE INVERT
    Answer: When he tried to hang wallpaper, she became—UNRAVELED

48. **Jumbles** SKULK HOUSE WHITEN BLOODY
Answer: When the fight was over, the boxer ended up licking—HIS WOUNDS

49. **Jumbles** ICING CASTE MILDEW WINTRY
Answer: Needed by the pretzel makers to increase sales—A NEW "TWIST"

50. **Jumbles** EMERY DOWDY FINITE WEAPON
Answer: The boss never closed his office door because he was—"OPEN" MINDED

51. **Jumbles** SPURN MAGIC WHINNY BEGONE
Answer: What the teenager experienced on the farm—"GROWING" PAINS

52. **Jumbles** JEWEL HABIT LAUNCH MOBILE
Answer: Where the assistant ended up when the door wouldn't fit—IN A "JAMB"

53. **Jumbles** VISOR VIRUS PURIFY CATTLE
Answer: What citizens turn into at tax time—"PAY-TRIOTS"

54. **Jumbles** FUZZY PROBE MARLIN TUXEDO
Answer: Often caused by a difficult word game—PUZZLEMENT

55. **Jumbles** CHALK QUASH PHYSIC IMBUED
Answer: What the movie star did when she dived into the pool—MADE A "SPLASH"

56. **Jumbles** FEIGN THICK POSTAL MALICE
Answer: When Grandma ran out of jars, she was—LEFT IN A "PICKLE"

57. **Jumbles** QUAIL ELOPE EROTIC FLORAL
Answer: What the hostess faced before the dinner party—A FULL PLATE

58. **Jumbles** HONEY LOVER SULTRY VORTEX
Answer: The carpenter was highly recommended because he was strictly—ON THE "LEVEL"

59. **Jumbles** VIPER LOUSE WHALER DECEIT
Answer: What she considered her first takeoff—A "DEPARTURE"

60. **Jumbles** RUMMY CRIME STODGY EFFACE
Answer: Why the young surgeon was hired—HE MADE THE "CUT"

61. **Jumbles** TWEET TEASE RATION BECALM
Answer: What the patrons were left with when the sweetshop raised prices—A "BITTER" TASTE

62. **Jumbles** CHASM AVAIL SLEEPY GATHER
Answer: What the coach did to the end who missed the catch—GAVE HIM A "PASS"

63. **Jumbles** FAINT FROZE MYRIAD MORGUE
Answer: Why the student got *D*s and *F*s—TOO MANY *Z*s

64. **Jumbles** HAVOC FIORD ASTHMA SCORCH
Answer: What the stranded campers used to stay warm—A "FIR" COAT

65. **Jumbles** LIBEL OUNCE DAWNED CHERUB
Answer: Studying culinary arts made him this—WELL "ROUNDED"

66. **Jumbles** CURVE DIZZY FRACAS GENDER
Answer: What the feuding workers did in the sugar fields—"RAZED" CAIN

67. **Jumbles** PURGE AGATE POLICY FLORID
Answer: Why he decided to change barbers—HE GOT "CLIPPED"

68. **Jumbles** REBEL FLOUR SUGARY MARROW
Answer: What the troops conducted during barracks cleanup—"GERM" WARFARE

69. **Jumbles** FETCH BIRCH ENDURE GULLET
Answer: After the victory, the pom-pom girls were—"CHEER" FULL

70. **Jumbles** BRAWL DROOP BOBBIN DELUXE
Answer: How the shipping clerk felt on an especially busy day—"BOXED" IN

71. **Jumbles** FAIRY LEAKY RENEGE EASILY
Answer: He hung up on the telemarketer because his sales pitch had a—FALSE "RING"

72. **Jumbles** SOUSE UPPER APATHY PICKET
Answer: What the timber boss took to work—HIS "CHOPPER"

73. **Jumbles** EXCEL CLOUT SAVORY POCKET
Answer: Hard to do when the air conditioner goes out on a hot day—KEEP YOUR "COOL"

74. **Jumbles** RIGOR OWING BUTTON FLAUNT
Answer: How close did the couple come to winning the dance contest?—A "FOOT" OR TWO

75. **Jumbles** AWARD BEGUN BODICE QUENCH
Answer: What the manager said when the club members played craps—"NO DICE"

76. **Jumbles** FOAMY HUSKY SOCKET OCCULT
Answer: The salesman gave the customer a hard sell because he was—A SOFT TOUCH

77. **Jumbles** LEAVE PAUSE CANDID MAYHEM
Answer: What the cosmetics saleswoman gave the mobster's wife—A "SHADY" DEAL

78. **Jumbles** HYENA LUCID FRUGAL INVITE
Answer: The aged housekeeper attributed her longevity to this—"CLEAN" LIVING

79. **Jumbles** EAGLE MAKER PULPIT WORTHY
Answer: What the busy executive finished over the weekend—HIS "PAPER" WORK

80. **Jumbles** GOING TANGY NINETY HUMBLE
Answer: Building a lamp in class was—"ENLIGHTENING"

81. **Jumbles** DAUNT BORAX FIDDLE VALISE
Answer: What the doctor considered his chief nurse—"FIRST AID"

82. **Jumbles** DRONE SCOUT VIRILE POWDER
Answer: The kind of argument often heard at a sports bar—A "SPIRITED" ONE

83. **Jumbles** WHISK VYING BABIED BLUISH
Answer: What the archeologist's friends admired when they saw the new house—HIS "DIGS"

84. **Jumbles** NEWSY SWAMP NEARLY ENTITY
Answer: The printer broke up with his girlfriend because she—WASN'T HIS "TYPE"

85. **Jumbles** TROTH YOUNG CALICO PAUNCH
Answer: What Dad turned into when the kids got too loud—A COUCH GROUCH

86. **Jumbles** HAREM QUOTA DOUBLE RADIAL
Answer: The wine steward showed the diner how to do this—HOLD HIS LIQUOR

87. **Jumbles** IVORY ALTAR CHEERY SWIVEL
Answer: What the combat pilots conducted when their uncle's will was read—AN HEIR WAR

88. **Jumbles** PROVE MINOR OUTBID BRONCO
Answer: Where the all-day conference was held—IN THE "BORED" ROOM

89. **Jumbles** SKIMP PANDA FIZZLE BRIDGE
Answer: When hubby raided the cookie jar, the astronomer said he was—THE BIG "DIPPER"

90. **Jumbles** FRANC CHAFE ENMITY UNPACK
Answer: What the cowboy got when he left his horse at the stable—A "REIN" CHECK

91. **Jumbles** UNIFY LOOSE LIZARD ZIGZAG
Answer: When he barbecued in the hot sun, he was—"SIZZLING"

92. **Jumbles** CAKED TRACT VERIFY DELUGE
Answer: What to do with an old broken bike—"RECYCLE" IT

93. **Jumbles** SKUNK BUILT DREDGE TOFFEE
Answer: When the fireman fell for the scam artist's pitch, he—GOT "BURNED"

94. **Jumbles** BROIL GROUP VASSAL NAPKIN
Answer: What Mom said when Dad spilled chowder on his shirt—"SOUP'S ON"

95. **Jumbles** IGLOO BYLAW ECZEMA AGHAST
Answer: What the ambitious tire salesman wanted to become—A BIG "WHEEL"

96. **Jumbles** EXULT COWER FERVOR HOTBED
Answer: Where the driver ended up when he got hot under the collar—IN THE COOLER

97. **Jumbles** IMPEL GOOSE BROGUE WOBBLE
Answer: What the football star looked forward to during the off-season—A SUPER "BOWL"

98. **Jumbles** AORTA KAPOK HANDLE ABDUCT
Answer: Why the diner didn't leave a tip—HE WAS OUT OF "BREAD"

99. **Jumbles** ELEGY MOOSE URCHIN ADRIFT
Answer: What the riflemen were told to do when the building started burning—CEASE "FIRE"

100. **Jumbles** BOOTH ASSAY BEAGLE DARING
Answer: Cotton can be this, except when it's picked—"ABSORBING"

101. **Jumbles** MURKY DOGMA PASTRY BARREL
Answer: What the brunettes left behind when they became blondes—THE "DARK" AGES

102. **Jumbles** KEYED HENCE CORRAL SAVAGE
Answer: Enjoyed by the young lottery winner long before his time—THE "GOLDEN" YEARS

103. **Jumbles** CUBIT FLOOR HALLOW FEWEST
Answer: What the portrait model gave the artist—THE "BRUSH-OFF"

104. **Jumbles** MEALY GLOVE FERVID PESTLE
Answer: Why the photo boss assigned the apprentice to the darkroom—TO "DEVELOP"

105. **Jumbles** LANKY HANDY LOCATE TURGID
Answer: What the highway foreman wanted the lazy worker to do—"HIT" THE ROAD

106. **Jumbles** CHIME FUSSY STOOGE WISELY
Answer: Getting on a scale in front of others can be a—"WEIGHTY" ISSUE

107. **Jumbles** INKED COMET JAUNTY SLOGAN
Answer: When the superstar couldn't find a seat on the bench, he was—OUT, STANDING

108. **Jumbles** MOUSE EIGHT PUNDIT KOSHER
Answer: Avoided by someone who's shallow-minded—DEEP THOUGHTS

109. **Jumbles** PATCH BRAIN AVENUE UNTRUE
Answer: The exterminator quit because he was tired of this—THE RAT RACE

110. **Jumbles** GRIMY SUEDE TETHER PREFER
Answer: Easy for a neckwear salesman to do before Father's Day—GET "TIED" UP

111. **Jumbles** LEAFY LOUSY CORNER HEARTH
Answer: A homemaker is often too busy for this—HERSELF

112. **Jumbles** SWASH EXACT SHANTY BREACH
Answer: When the fish house offered free meals, the couple asked—"WHAT'S THE "CATCH"?

113. **Jumbles** BURST ABASH ACHING HAWKER
Answer: What the recycling firm generated—TRASH CASH

114. **Jumbles** SNORT CLEFT MOROSE NIPPLE
Answer: What the fortune-teller turned into on vacation—A SITE "SEER"

115. **Jumbles** PIKER CHAMP FICKLE SCENIC
Answer: What the director ended up with when he filmed the barnyard scene—A "CHICK" FLICK

116. **Jumbles** AWOKE MONEY UNCURL KOWTOW
Answer: What the busy violinist was up to—HIS NECK IN WORK

117. **Jumbles** TOPAZ IDIOM FIXING WALRUS
Answer: The young candidate was elected because he was—"PROMISING"

118. **Jumbles** COCOA STOIC BEETLE CAVORT
Answer: What the saloon keeper took when the cowboys got rowdy—"COVER"

119. **Jumbles** HUMID VAGUE ABSORB INNING
Answer: Mountain climbers will do this while they rest—HANG AROUND

120. **Jumbles** FLUKE MINCE SONATA GOPHER
Answer: Eating chocolate chips in bed can create this—A COOKIE "SHEET"

121. **Jumbles** DOUSE BASIS CANKER PSYCHE
Answer: His piano studies led him to the—"KEYS" TO SUCCESS

122. **Jumbles** MADAM GAWKY HEARSE EMBARK
Answer: What Dad faced when the family went for a drive—AHEAD

123. **Jumbles** CHAOS TONIC CRAFTY BAKERY
Answer: What the comedian made when his car hit the building—A NASTY "CRACK"

124. **Jumbles** DRYLY BLAZE MEMOIR SAFARI
Answer: When the train conductor went surfing, it was—ALL A "BOARD"

125. **Jumbles** AMITY MAJOR HEREBY NOODLE
Answer: What last night put an end to—ANOTHER DAY

126. **Jumbles** PANIC GRAIN ASSAIL KISMET
Answer: What she faced when she started her diet—"SLIM" PICKINGS

127. **Jumbles** VALVE HOVEL LARYNX VIABLE
Answer: How the planetarium worker described his work—"HEAVENLY"

128. **Jumbles** GRAVE VOCAL PARISH FILLET
Answer: What the soprano ended up with when she got a sore throat—A "FEVER" PITCH

129. **Jumbles** DRAMA RODEO CEMENT HINDER
Answer: What the leather-maker did on vacation—"TANNED" HIS HIDE

130. **Jumbles** OZONE CRESS AUTUMN BELFRY
Answer: What the sailors ended up with when the ship ran aground—A SEA OF TROUBLE

131. **Jumbles** OCTET SUAVE FACTOR MALADY
Answer: Why she splurged on the shoes—A SALE WAS AFOOT

132. **Jumbles** CHICK ALBUM ENCORE ANSWER
Answer: What he ended up with when he drove after some drinks—A "CHASER"

133. **Jumbles** COUPE BIPED ADJUST JABBER
Answer: Buying a new car left him—SCARED TO "DEBT"

134. **Jumbles** WEARY PARTY BEAVER MALTED
Answer: Why the seer visited the library—TO "READ" BETTER

135. **Jumbles** FAVOR POUND VERMIN REDEEM
Answer: What the cowboys did with the herd of cattle—DROVE THE DROVE

136. **Jumbles** HAZEL TOKEN HARROW TAWDRY
Answer: What the bricklayer did when she changed her mind—THREW IN THE TROWEL

137. **Jumbles** EXUDE JUMBO DROPSY MAKEUP
Answer: When business went down at the music store, he—"DRUMMED" IT UP

138. **Jumbles** CROWN LAPEL KILLER FORAGE
Answer: What the musicians experienced in the stormy sea—ROCK AND ROLL

139. **Jumbles** PRIOR BURLY ACCEDE GAMBOL
Answer: When the struggling artist didn't sell his work, he said it was—HIS "BLUE" PERIOD

140. **Jumbles** BRIBE IRONY GLANCE UPTOWN
Answer: What the deep thinker focused on when he bought a large-screen TV—THE "BIG PICTURE"

141. **Jumbles** FORUM AHEAD SQUALL GUITAR
Answer: When the female impersonator prepared for the show, it was—QUITE A "DRAG"

142. **Jumbles** EXPEL MOUSY GRISLY CRAYON
Answer: What it cost the king to educate his sons—"PRINCELY" SUMS

143. **Jumbles** CHANT FIFTY PRAYER BEACON
Answer: Where the tree trimmer applied for the bank loan—THE "BRANCH" OFFICE

144. **Jumbles** BRIAR GNOME CALLOW BROKEN
Answer: What the kids turned the den into on a rainy day—A "WRECK" ROOM

145. **Jumbles** GUILE UNCAP SLOUCH GOITER
Answer: When the ump dialed his wife on their anniversary, he made—THE RIGHT "CALL"

146. **Jumbles** KNIFE USURP INTAKE DIGEST
Answer: What sis did when Junior played with her perfume—RAISED A "STINK"

147. **Jumbles** ANNOY KNEEL BYGONE HUNTER
Answer: What Dad ended up with when he put on his golf socks—A "HOLE IN ONE"

148. **Jumbles** BLANK FLOUT STYLUS BOYISH
Answer: What the bartender offered the achy, feverish customer—A FLU "SHOT"

149. **Jumbles** MAXIM RAJAH INVENT FALTER
Answer: No longer included in the airfare—AIR "FARE"

150. **Jumbles** CHAFF VIXEN PALLID BRUTAL
Answer: What the scientist wanted to do after the earthquake—FIND "FAULT"

151. **Jumbles** HAVEN SYLPH BUCKLE NUTRIA
Answer: When the pupil completed his punishment, he ended up with—A CLEAN "SLATE"

152. **Jumbles** ALIAS MOLDY BICEPS NIMBLE
Answer: What happened when the store reduced the price of ladders—SALES "CLIMBED"

153. **Jumbles** TYING FUDGE SOIREE MARTYR
Answer: When the police chief announced his crime crackdown, his remarks were—"ARRESTING"

154. **Jumbles** FATAL CLUCK IRONIC ALKALI
Answer: What the actor made backstage—A CURTAIN "CALL"

155. **Jumbles** SILKY CHEEK JACKET TURNIP
Answer: Why the banker fired the loan officer—LACK OF "INTEREST"

156. **Jumbles** TWICE EPOCH PIRATE SHREWD
Answer: What the class considered the driving instructor's dog—TEACHER'S "PET"

157. **Jumbles** CLOVE PEONY THORAX NOVICE
Answer: Needed before the cement truck arrives—A "CONCRETE" PLAN

158. **Jumbles** LIMIT SOAPY MOTION BECAME
Answer: What she was fishing for on vacation—"COMPLIMENTS"

159. **Jumbles** AZURE FLUID MUSTER SMUDGE
Answer: How he felt when a sudden wind blew a tree down on his car—"DIS-GUSTED"

160. **Jumbles** AROMA PRONE NUMBER BENUMB
Answer: What a golfer will do on a rainy Saturday—MOURN THE MORN

161. **Jumbles** JUNIOR FORGER HUNGRY SALUTE ASTRAY FRIGID
Answer: What they did when they visited the Grand Canyon—"GORGED" ON THE SIGHTS

162. **Jumbles** INLAND FLABBY PLOWED BLOUSE TRICKY PENMAN
Answer: She couldn't make a good cup of coffee because she—DIDN'T KNOW "BEANS"

163. **Jumbles** PALATE GENIUS SURELY MOHAIR TAUGHT LAGOON
Answer: When the joke bombed, the theater manager said it was no—LAUGHING MATTER

164. **Jumbles** AWHILE RUBBER DEMISE FELLOW MUFFIN DECODE
Answer: When he flunked the vocabulary test—WORDS FAILED HIM

165. **Jumbles** CANOPY PIGEON UNLOCK CONVEX NORMAL TUMULT
Answer: Why the track star missed his flight—HE WAS "RUNNING" LATE

166. **Jumbles** CANYON GRASSY ADROIT WEASEL TIDBIT LEVITY
Answer: A bunch of beer bellies can turn a bar into this—A VAST "WAIST-LAND"

167. **Jumbles** BECKON FROSTY OPENLY LEAVEN BECOME UNEASY
Answer: What the famous author did when he gave a lecture—HE SPOKE "VOLUMES"

168. **Jumbles** WHENCE LICHEN SIMILE HECTIC TUSSLE GHETTO
Answer: What the eye doctor wanted his new location ad to do—CITE SIGHT SITE

169. **Jumbles** MIDDAY INWARD DUPLEX FIASCO SHADOW BELONG
Answer: The tattoo artist got the job because he made—A GOOD "IMPRESSION"

170. **Jumbles** TOTTER OXYGEN OUTFIT PILLAR PREFIX INVEST
Answer: What the leading man got when he was divorced—A "SUPPORTING" ROLE

171. **Jumbles** TACKLE TORRID BOTTLE EITHER CUDGEL EXHALE
Answer: Heard at a bus stop on a cold, snowy night—"CHATTER" CHATTER

172. **Jumbles** TRUANT BUNION MARKUP GYRATE PAGODA OVERDO
Answer: What the class did when they visited the primate house—"MONKEYED" AROUND

173. **Jumbles** FACIAL MODIFY ARCTIC FLAXEN MUSEUM PARLOR
Answer: When he rode the merry-go-round with his son, Dad said he had—COME FULL "CIRCLE"

174. **Jumbles** ABRUPT LAYOFF PRISON MAROON CODGER BISHOP
Answer: The young trucker depended on the dispatcher because he was—A "ROADS" SCHOLAR

175. **Jumbles** DOUBLY INFANT YELLOW HOMAGE PATTER ABSURD
Answer: The mogul invested in the nursery because it was a—"GROWTH" INDUSTRY

176. **Jumbles** INFLUX TYPHUS EQUITY CARBON HOOKUP GIGOLO
Answer: When the crochet class met in a smaller room, they became a—CLOSE-KNIT GROUP

177. **Jumbles** GEYSER SNITCH COHORT ITALIC COUPON NATURE
Answer: The student turned his rail ride into a—"TRAIN" OF THOUGHT

178. **Jumbles** UNIQUE MELODY JAGGED LIQUID ARTFUL UPWARD
Answer: The professor scolded the violin students because they—"FIDDLED" AROUND

179. **Jumbles** MISHAP COMPEL DRAGON EYEFUL BELIEF SPRUCE
Answer: What the beauty queen turned into when she addressed the crowd—A "FIGURE" OF SPEECH

180. **Jumbles** ENTICE PICNIC EYELID BOUNCE SOLACE FUSION
Answer: The divorce judge gave the boxer a—"SPLIT" DECISION

187

Need More Jumbles®?

Jumble® Books

More than 175 puzzles each!

Animal Jumble®
$9.95 • ISBN: 1-57243-197-0

Jammin' Jumble®
$9.95 • ISBN: 1-57243-844-4

Jazzy Jumble®
$9.95 • ISBN: 978-1-57243-962-7

Joyful Jumble®
$9.95 • ISBN: 978-1-60078-079-0

Juke Joint Jumble®
$9.95 • ISBN: 978-1-60078-295-4

Jumble® at Work
$9.95 • ISBN: 1-57243-147-4

Jumble® Celebration
$9.95 • ISBN: 978-1-60078-134-6

Jumble® Explosion
$9.95 • ISBN: 978-1-60078-078-3

Jumble® Fever
$9.95 • ISBN: 1-57243-593-3

Jumble® Fiesta
$9.95 • ISBN: 1-57243-626-3

Jumble® Fun
$9.95 • ISBN: 1-57243-379-5

Jumble® Genius
$9.95 • ISBN: 1-57243-896-7

Jumble® Grab Bag
$9.95 • ISBN: 1-57243-273-X

Jumble® Jackpot
$9.95 • ISBN: 1-57243-897-5

Jumble® Jambalaya
$9.95 • ISBN: 978-1-60078-294-7

Jumble® Jamboree
$9.95 • ISBN: 1-57243-696-4

Jumble® Jubilee
$9.95 • ISBN: 1-57243-231-4

Jumble® Juggernaut
$9.95 • ISBN: 978-1-60078-026-4

Jumble® Junction
$9.95 • ISBN: 1-57243-380-9

Jumble® Jungle
$9.95 • ISBN: 978-1-57243-961-0

Jumble® Madness
$9.95 • ISBN: 1-892049-24-4

Jumble® Mania
$9.95 • ISBN: 1-57243-697-2

Jumble® See & Search
$9.95 • ISBN: 1-57243-549-6

Jumble® See & Search 2
$9.95 • ISBN: 1-57243-734-0

Jumble® Surprise
$9.95 • ISBN: 1-57243-320-5

Jumpin' Jumble®
$9.95 • ISBN: 978-1-60078-027-1

Ready, Set, Jumble®
$9.95 • ISBN: 978-1-60078-133-0

Sports Jumble®
$9.95 • ISBN: 1-57243-113-X

Summer Fun Jumble®
$9.95 • ISBN: 1-57243-114-8

Travel Jumble®
$9.95 • ISBN: 1-57243-198-9

TV Jumble®
$9.95 • ISBN: 1-57243-461-9

Oversize Jumble® Books

More than 500 puzzles each!

Colossal Jumble®
$19.95 • ISBN: 1-57243-490-2

Generous Jumble®
$19.95 • ISBN: 1-57243-385-X

Giant Jumble®
$19.95 • ISBN: 1-57243-349-3

Gigantic Jumble®
$19.95 • ISBN: 1-57243-426-0

Jumbo Jumble®
$19.95 • ISBN: 1-57243-314-0

The Very Best of Jumble® BrainBusters
$19.95 • ISBN: 1-57243-845-2

Jumble® Crosswords™

More than 175 puzzles each!

Jumble® Crosswords™
$9.95 • ISBN: 1-57243-347-7

More Jumble® Crosswords™
$9.95 • ISBN: 1-57243-386-8

Jumble® Crosswords™ Adventure
$9.95 • ISBN: 1-57243-462-7

Jumble® Crosswords™ Challenge
$9.95 • ISBN: 1-57243-423-6

Jumble® Crosswords™ Jackpot
$9.95 • ISBN: 1-57243-615-8

Jumble® Crosswords™ Jamboree
$9.95 • ISBN: 1-57243-787-1

Jumble® BrainBusters™

More than 175 puzzles each!

Jumble® BrainBusters™
$9.95 • ISBN: 1-892049-28-7

Jumble® BrainBusters™ II
$9.95 • ISBN: 1-57243-424-4

Jumble® BrainBusters™ III
$9.95 • ISBN: 1-57243-463-5

Jumble® BrainBusters™ IV
$9.95 • ISBN: 1-57243-489-9

Jumble® BrainBusters™ 5
$9.95 • ISBN: 1-57243-548-8

Hollywood Jumble® BrainBusters™
$9.95 • ISBN: 1-57243-594-1

Jumble® BrainBusters™ Bonanza
$9.95 • ISBN: 1-57243-616-6

Boggle™ BrainBusters™
$9.95 • ISBN: 1-57243-592-5

Boggle™ BrainBusters™ 2
$9.95 • ISBN: 1-57243-788-X

Jumble® BrainBusters™ Junior
$9.95 • ISBN: 1-892049-29-5

Jumble® BrainBusters™ Junior II
$9.95 • ISBN: 1-57243-425-2

Fun in the Sun with Jumble® BrainBusters™
$9.95 • ISBN: 1-57243-733-2